ON THE OUTSKIRTS

Michael Frayn

ON THE OUTSKIRTS

Collins ST JAMES'S PLACE · LONDON · 1964

All the pieces in this book appeared originally in
my column in 'The Observer', and are reproduced
here by arrangement with the Editor

Contents

New Man Coming

One's personality is a remarkably stable structure; and the most stable element in it is one's steadfast conviction that it is just on the point of being entirely transformed.

Transformed, needless to say, not by any efforts of one's own, but by magic objects and events outside oneself. One's dissatisfactions and limitations will be suddenly and wonderfully sloughed off, one comes to believe, when one has acquired a striped suit, or a red car; when one has got married; when one has written a book, or found God, or learnt Italian; when one has reached the age of 10; when one has moved house; when summer comes.

It is strange that so much of one's action is motivated by such patent witchcraft. But in a society where unhappiness is regarded rather like fleas, as an unappealing state people ought to be ashamed of getting into, I suppose it is congenial to see oneself as a naturally happy soul hindered from achieving perfect contentment only by external causes. All these extraordinary superstitions are ways of concealing from oneself the painful fact that most of one's discontents are the inevitable by-products of one's own nature.

I rely a bit on almost all these superstitions, but most particularly on those that involve straightforward covetousness. If I had a certain material object, I have repeatedly felt, my whole life would be entirely changed. From its small corner the totem would radiate such a powerful field of rightness and delight that everything else would come to glow in sympathy.

The first thing I can remember coveting as a child was a propelling pencil that wrote in five colours, after I had seen the teacher correcting exercise books with one. Other little

7

boys might have conceived a passion for the teacher, but I fell in love with the propelling pencil. It was beautiful, and I desired it. The provocative glimpses of the coloured leads through the slots in the side inflamed my senses. I longed to touch the exquisite texture of the nickel-plating.

My parents were driven to say they would buy me one— but, torment of hopes raised only to be the more savagely hurled down, there was none in the shops! I raged about the house like a tiny junkie deprived of his fix, while they ransacked London, and after days of great misery for all of us, ran one to earth in far-off Peckham Rye. But so supremely unimportant did it become as soon as I possessed it that I cannot even remember what happened to it.

It sometimes seems to me that the whole story of my life could be adequately told in the catalogue of my love affairs. There was the affair with the ten-and-sixpenny plastic crystal set (purchased—never worked); the affair with the miniature starting-pistol (owned by a friend—fiercely desired through long centuries of time—swapped for about half my possessions —instantly devalued, and allowed to fall to pieces before it could fire the five blank cartridges which my friend's father was keeping locked up to celebrate the end of the war with); the affair with the second-hand sports car (£180—"Take you anywhere, that car," said the salesman, "Take you to Land's End and back,") snatched away at the last moment by a providential failure to raise the money.

One learns, of course. I don't think I shall ever fall in love with another propelling pencil, or another plastic crystal set. But the inoculation is against the particular ju-jus I've tried, not against ju-jus in general. It doesn't in any way deter me from my present mania, for example, which is coveting a swivel chair. If I had a swivel chair, upholstered in worn leather, I *know* I should be a new man.

I can see myself very clearly with the swivel chair. I am a calm man, a responsible man, a happy man, a man who can work for eight hours at a stretch without being interrupted by fatigue, boredom, bad temper or incompetence, a man who can take well-earned relaxation with his smiling wife and laughing child in some gay but uplifting leisure pursuit. I am a man who keeps an exquisitely selected early June day permanently outside his window. I am a man who does not get telephone calls from people who think they are phoning the South Eastern Gas Board.

I am a man who is swinging gently from side to side in his worn leather swivel chair as he decides whether to spend the sunlit working day ahead on finishing his play about the ultimate essence of man, or starting the essay in which the ultimate nature of the universe is set forth in 500 exact and simple words.

Manufacturers of swivel chairs, join me in happy contemplation of the picture! Sooner or later I shall have the swivel chair, and you will have the money for it. How would you ever sell me a swivel chair I do not need if I did not believe I was buying a complete new personality? How would any five-colour propelling pencils ever be sold if other people did not share my disorder? How would the evangelists and the travel agents survive?

And just as surely as I know the man in the swivel chair will be a new and perfect man, so I know he will be the same inadequate one, not only depressed by the weather, interrupted by the telephone, unable to find a pen that works, and confused about exactly what he is supposed to be doing, but also driven to final exasperation because the swivel on the blasted chair is broken.

I know it only too well. Perhaps it's just as well for all concerned that I don't actually believe it.

9

Hamlet OBE

The one heavy industry that shows no sign of declining is the vast enterprise which turns all that crude Shakespeare the country possesses into finished Peter Hall and Peter Brook.

I sometimes wonder if the workers in this industry ever worry lest one day they exhaust all the possible permutations of interpretation, editing, punctuation, fancy dress, and general joking up, and find themselves reduced to the shameful expedient of putting the stuff on more or less as the old fool wrote it.

I'm not *advocating* this; I couldn't sit through a *Hamlet* uncut and unrelieved by cheering breaks for swordplay. All the same, as time goes on the variations left to try are going to become pretty esoteric. Particularly when the National Foundation Stone on the South Bank gets under way with all the brainpower at its command.

They may bulk the programme out with *Roots, Look Back in Anger, The Caretaker, Roots* done in Second Empire costume, *Look Back in Anger* in Gestapo uniforms and riding boots, *The Caretaker* in Melanesian ritual masks, *Roots* chanted by antiphonal choruses of Manchester schoolgirls, *Look Back in Anger* danced to music by Chopin and Rachmaninov, *The Caretaker* mimed by actors from the Kabuki Theatre, and so on and so forth, but in between whiles it's going to be Shakespeare, Shakespear, Shaksper.

By the end of the century they should be very far out indeed. Here's a preview of what Lord Olivier of Elstree,

Sir Kenneth Tynan, Sir Sean Kenny, Sir Lionel Bart, Bart., and Dame Kayser Bondor will be giving us for the winter season of 1999—*Hamlet, O.B.E.*

ACT ONE

[*Enter Ghost, in phosphorescent buskins.*]
Horatio: Look! My! Lord, it comes!
[*He flexes his thighs.*]
Hamlet: Angels and ministers of grace defend us!
[*While the Ghost mimes telling his tale, angels and ministers of grace appear dressed as fighter-pilots and Ministers of Defence and burlesque defending us in a satirical anti-war masque.*]
Ghost: Adieu, adieu! Hamlet, remember me.
[*Exit, pursued by a bear.*]
Hamlet: O that! This too? Too solid!
      Flesh would melt,
         Thaw—and resolve itself in two.
            Adieu!
[*He slaps his buskins.*]
Ophelia: O! what a noble! Mind is here o'erthrown!
[*They fight.*]

ACT TWO

[*Hamlet, Horatio, Laertes, and attendant Knights Commander. They flex their thighs and slap their buskins.*]
Hamlet: How long hast thou been grave, mucker?
[*The grave diggers perform a very grave digging dance, while newsreel shots of the assassination of Archduke Ferdinand are shown in back projection.*]

11

Hamlet: The play's the thing
           Wherein I'll slap the buskins of the king.
[*They fight.*]

ACT THREE

[*Another part of the plot. The King, Rosencrantz, Guildenstern,
etc. They flex their buskins and slap their thighs.*]
Polonius [*aside*]: Though this be madness, yet there is Method
  in't.
[*They fight.*]

ACT FOUR

Hamlet: To be or not.
           To be *that*
           Is the question whether.
[*He thighs, and busks his slapkins. They fight.*]

ACT FIVE

Hamlet: The rest is silence.
[*Dies.*]
Horatio: Now cracks a noble.
[*A noble cracks. Horatio auscults him.*]
                                              Heart good.
[*Yawning, and offering a chocolate to Fortinbras.*]
                                  'Night! Sweet, Prince?
Fortinbras: Let four captains
               Bear *Hamlet*, like a soldier, from the stage;

For it was likely, had it been put on,
To have prov'd most royally.
[*A dead march. Exeunt, bearing knighthoods.*]

I said, "My Name Is 'Ozzy' Manders, Dean of King's"

I must not tell lies.

I must not tell pointless lies.

I must not tell pointless lies at parties.

I must not tell pointless lies at parties when they are plainly going to be found out in the next 10 minutes.

I must not:

1. Let it be thought that I have caught the name of anyone I am ever introduced to, because statistics show that I have never caught anyone's name until I have heard it at least 12 times.

2. Give it to be understood that I have already heard of the owner of the inaudible name, because tests show that apart from one or two obvious exceptions like William Shakespeare and Sir Harold Sidewinder I haven't heard of anyone.

3. Say I have read the man's books, or admired his architecture, or used his firm's brake-linings, or seen his agency's advertisements, or always been interested in his field of research, or know his home town, because I do hereby make a solemn and unconditional declaration, being before witnesses and in sober realisation of my past wrongdoing, that I have done none of these things.

4. Say that I know any of the people he is sure I must know, or have heard of any of the names he takes to be common knowledge, because I don't and haven't, or if I do and have, I've got them all hopelessly mixed up, and when he says Appel I'm thinking of Riopelle, and when he says Buffet I'm thinking of Dubuffet, and when he says Palma I'm thinking of

Palermo, and when he says syncretism I'm thinking of syndicalism, and when he says a man called "Pop" Tuddenham who hired a barrage balloon and dressed it up to look like an elephant I'm thinking of a man called "Tubby" Poppleton who hired a horse and dressed it up to look like the Senior Tutor.

5. Try to sustain the fiction that I have heard anything he has said to me over the noise, because I have not, and because he has heard nothing I have said, either, so that by analogy he *knows* I am lying just as surely as I know he is lying.

6. Bend my lips in an attempt to counterfeit a smile unless I am absolutely assured by the raising of a flag with the word JOKE on it that the man has made a joke and not announced that his mother has died.

7. In short, get involved in any more conversations that go:

"I've long been a great admirer of your, er . . . stuff, Mr. . . . er . . . er . . . "

"*How kind of you.*"

"Oh, all kinds."

"*No, I'm afraid some critics haven't been at all kind.*"

"The tall kind? I see. I see."

(A long silence. I think.)

"I particularly liked your last boo . . . er, pla . . . , um, one."

"*Last what?*"

"One."

"*One what?*"

"Um, thing you, well, did."

"*Really? The Press panned it.*"

" 'The Press Bandit'—of course, it was on the tip of my tongue."

"*Well, the Irish banned it.*"

"I mean 'The Irish Bandit,' of course. How stupid of me."

15

"*But everyone else panned it.*"

"Oh, Elsie Pandit. You mean *Mrs.* Pandit?"

"*Who*—your *missus panned it?*"

"No, India's Mrs. Pandit."

"*They panned it in India, too, did they?*"

"Did they? I suppose Mrs. Pandit banned it."

"*Ah. You know India, do you?*"

"No. You do, do you?"

"*No.*"

"Ah."

"*Hm.*"

(I smile a cryptic, knowing smile. He smiles a cryptic, knowing smile. We are getting on wonderfully. Just then my wife comes up and wants to be introduced, and I have to ask the man who he is.)

Why do I do these things? Do I think the man's going to give me a fiver, or a year's free supply of his works, for having heard of his name? Do I think he's going to twist my arm and kick me on the kneecap if I don't like his stuff? He doesn't *expect* me to like it. No one likes it except his wife and the editor of *Spasm* and 780 former pupils of F. R. Leavis. Anyway, I've got him mixed up with someone else, and he didn't do it, and even what he didn't do isn't what I think he did. For heaven's sake, am *I* going to strike *him* because he thinks I'm called Freen, and that I write articles for the Lord's Day Observance Society?

I must not waste my valuable talent for deceit on lies which have no conceivable purpose when I could be saving it up for lies which would show a cash return.

I must instead say "I'm sorry, I didn't quite catch your name."

I must say "I'm sorry, I still haven't quite . . ."

I must say "I'm sorry—did you say 'Green' or 'Queen'?

16

Ah. Queen who? Come again . . . Queen *Elizabeth?* Elizabeth what?"

I must say "I expect I should know, but I'm afraid I don't— what do you do? I beg your pardon? Rain? You study it, do you—rainfall statistics and so on? No? You rain? You mean you actually rain yourself? I see. I see."

I must say "No, I *don't* see. What do you mean, you rain . . . ?"

I must . . .

I must not, on second thoughts, be pointlessly honest, either. . . .

Superb Views, Central Heating Throughout

A Channel tunnel would be better than a Channel bridge. The death penalty ought to be abolished. Visconti is a good but not a great director. Flying is pleasanter than travelling by train. . . . Well, I could go on all night: I believe I have one of the most extensive collections of opinions in the country.

They're a wonderful thing to collect, opinions. Putting them together demands no time, effort, or specialised knowledge, and they take up less space than stamps or bus-tickets. They're very sociable things to have, too. You can swap them with a stranger to break the ice. You can bring them out when your relations call. They make a party go. And, of course, they're absolutely safe.

Let me show you some more of mine. What would you like? Public schools, Southern Rhodesia, Norman Mailer, galoshes, Hungarian cooking? Take one—I've got stacks. How about one on Norma Talmadge, unofficial strikes, or Zadar as an unspoilt holiday centre? No, go on—they don't cost me anything, after all.

That's what I like about opinions. Anyone can afford to have opinions about anything. When you have an opinion you forget the nagging worries and insoluble difficulties in your everyday life and move into a world where everything can be neatly and rationally arranged. And some of the opinions one has are very striking. You'd be amazed at some of mine. I suppose the really important thing about them is that they express one's personality. I mean, if I say I'm against nuclear war, that doesn't in any way weaken the country's defences, but it does tell you what a fundamentally decent, left-wing sort of chap I am.

I'll tell you another thing I like about opinions. They're very good for your soul. They deflect your attention away from yourself and your problems towards the problems of others. I mean, I've no opinion at all on how to organise my own life, or what to do about the armchair leg that seceded from the armchair last week. But I have perfectly simple and definite opinions on how everyone else ought to behave, and what to do about the secession of Katanga. Isn't that wonderful?

What would you like an opinion on now? String? String vests? String quartets? String beans? String pulling? Let's do an exchange. I'll swap my opinion on divorce law reform for yours on Saul Bellow. I need an opinion on Saul Bellow to complete a set I'm collecting on Modern American Novelists.

What do you think about musique concrète, incidentally? Do you like the Seagram Building? Now we're well launched on to art, you see. What a useful adjunct to opinion-collecting art is! In fact, the whole point of art, I believe, is to have opinions about it. Works of art are hollow spaces defined by the opinions that gather round them. With what relief we turn from contemplating the inscrutable hole in the middle to the solid opinions all round. *The last act seems forced and structurally unsound but. The slow movement is full of a typical sardonic gloom which.* Thank God, something to agree or disagree with! In fact, enjoying art is exchanging opinions about it. I mean, correct me if I'm wrong. One might even ask what value or reality an opinion itself can have except in so far as it is the subject of another opinion.

Come on, opine away. The preservation of the white rhinoceros, the morals of "Lolita," the aesthetics of braces. . . . Don't let the conversation flag.

After all, this is what one's education is for. Ask someone

19

who hasn't had the benefit of a liberal education what he thinks of Cavafy and he might well be stumped. Not me, though. "I can't stand him," I should say with a slight, apologetic smile. I haven't read a word of Cavafy, either, but far from letting that slow me down I should turn it to good account. "I can't read him," I should say with devastating finality. "I simply cannot read him."

It's good exercise for one's intellect, holding opinions. It's healthy exercise for one's emotions to hold the sort of opinions that come trimmed with moral indignation—they cost no more than the ordinary sort. What a warm, healthy glow right-wing commentators give off when the United Nations troops shoot down unarmed civilians in Katanga! How the blood pulses bravely in the veins of us on the left when Katangan mercenaries do the same! In fact, when you come to think how enjoyable and health-giving moral indignation is, it makes you wonder whether the injustice and suffering that gave rise to it can really be such unrelievedly bad things after all.

There are all sorts of things we might live without. But what would life be like without opinion? What is a man, after all, but the sum of his opinions? What purpose has he, or any of his works, but to be the subject of opinions in others?

I wonder that opinion is not more frankly worshipped. I should like to see it personified in our working mythology as Opinia, a mature figure bearing reservations on the one hand and a glass of sherry in the other, with an interested smile, and with War, Pestilence, and Death peeping shyly from behind her skirts.

Then at least we should have someone to whom we could reasonably pray to be spared from participation, decision, and action.

Through the Wilderness

It is nice now that all you boys have got cars of your own (*said Mother*). You know how much it means to me when the three of you drive down to see me like this, and we can all have a good old chatter together.

John: That's right, Mother. So, as I was saying, Howard, I came down today through Wroxtead and Sudstow.

Howard: Really? I always come out through Dorris Hill and West Hatcham.

Ralph: I find I tend to turn off at the traffic lights in Manor Park Road myself and follow the 43 bus route through to the White Hart at Broylesden.

Mother: Ralph always was the adventurous one.

John: Last time I tried forking right just past the police station in Broylesden High Street. I wasn't very impressed with it as a route, though.

Howard: Weren't you? That's interesting. I've occasionally tried cutting through the Broylesden Heath Estate. Then you can either go along Mottram Road South or Creese End Broadway. I think it's handy to have the choice.

Ralph: Of course, much the prettiest way for my money is to carry on into Hangmore and go down past the pickles factory in Sunnydeep Lane.

Mother: Your father and I once saw Lloyd George going down Sunnydeep Lane in a *wheelbarrow*. . . .

Howard: Did you, Mother? I'm not very keen on the Sunnydeep Lane way personally. I'm a great believer in turning up Hangmore Hill and going round by the pre-fabs on the Common.

Ralph: Yes, yes, there's something to be said for that, too. What was the traffic like in Sudstow, then, John?

John: Getting a bit sticky.

Howard: Yes, it was getting a bit sticky in Broylesden. How was it in Dorris Hill, Ralph?

Ralph: Sticky, pretty sticky.

Mother: The traffic's terrible round here now. There was a most frightful accident yesterday just outside when . . .

Howard: Oh, you're bound to get them in traffic like this. Bound to.

Ralph: Where did you strike the traffic in Sudstow, then, John?

John: At the lights by the railway bridge. Do you know where I mean?

Ralph: Just by that dance hall where they had the trouble?

John: No, no. Next to the neon sign advertising mattresses.

Howard: Oh, you mean by the caravan depot? Just past Acme Motors?

John: Acme Motors? You're getting mixed up with Heaslam Road, Surley.

Howard: I'm pretty sure I'm not, you know.

John: I think you are, you know.

Howard: I don't think I am, you know.

John: Anyway, that's where I struck the traffic.

Ralph: I had a strange experience the other day.

John: Oh, really?

Ralph: I turned left at the lights in Broylesden High Street and cut down round the back of Coalpit Road. Thought I'd come out by the Wemblemore Palais. But what do you think happened? I came out by a new parade of shops, and I thought, hello, this must be Old Hangmore. Then I passed an Odeon—

John: An Odeon? In Old Hangmore?

22

Ralph: —and I thought, that's strange, there's no Odeon in Old Hangmore. Do you know where I was? In *New* Hangmore!

Howard: Getting lost in New Hangmore's nothing. I got lost last week in Upsome!

John: I went off somewhere into the blue only yesterday not a hundred yards from Sunnydeep Lane!

Mother: I remember I once got lost in the most curious circumstances in Singapore. . . .

Ralph: Anybody could get lost in Singapore, Mother.

John: To become personal for a moment, Howard, how's your car?

Howard: Not so bad, thanks, not so bad. And yours?

John: Not so bad, you know. How's yours, Ralph?

Ralph: Oh, not so bad, not so bad at all.

Mother: I had another of my turns last week.

Howard: We're talking about cars, Mother, CARS.

Mother: Oh, I'm sorry.

John: To change the subject a bit—you know where Linden Green Lane comes out, just by Upsome Quadrant?

Howard: Where Tunstall Road joins the Crescent there?

Ralph: Just by the Nervous Diseases Hospital?

John: That's right. Where the new roundabout's being built.

Howard: Almost opposite a truss shop with a giant model of a rupture belt outside?

Ralph: Just before you get to the bus station?

Howard: By the zebra crossing there?

John: That's right. Well, I had a puncture there on Friday.

Ralph: Well, then, I suppose we ought to think about getting back.

Howard: I thought I might turn off by the paint factory on the by-pass this time and give the Apex roundabout a miss.

John: Have either of you tried taking that side road at Tillotsons' Corner?

Ralph: There's a lot to be said for both ways. A lot to be said.

Mother: I'll go and make the tea while you discuss it, then. I know you've got more important things to do than sit here listening to an old woman like me chattering away all afternoon.

And Home's Son's Father is Hume's Father's Son

What a dynamic start! In the first six days of his ministry Sir Alec Douglas-Home has got rid of an earldom, three lordships, and two baronies; and the new Chancellor of the Duchy of Lancaster and the new Minister of State at the Board of Trade have acquired a viscountcy and a barony respectively.

Meanwhile, at the Conservative Central Office Lord Spoon is trying to drop the Barony of Spoon and pick up the Barony of Bosworth, to complete a set of "Battle" class titles he is collecting. "If I can send in the full set, together with the backs of three old Burke's 'Peerages,' I shall win an electric blanket," he told a Press conference late last night.

This vigorous programme cannot, of course, be carried through without some hard rethinking of fundamentals.

At the request of the Garter King-of-Arms, according to the *Daily Telegraph*, the Queen's advisers have been "urgently" considering the question of style and precedence of the former Lord Home's family. A spokesman for the College of Arms told the *Telegraph*: "The question is, for the purpose of precedence, whether the children of peers who have disclaimed are still children of peers."

How the College of Arms faced the problem I don't know, but its rather more venerable rival, the College of Arms and Legges (the name is a corruption of *armorum leges*, the laws of arms), responded with great promptitude. As soon as the urgency and gravity of the question was fully understood, an emergency meeting was called. Members of the College were rushed to London with police escorts, and a jet airliner was specially diverted to bring the Dexter Lord of Legges back from Southern Rhodesia, where he was inspecting pre-war baronetcies for signs of wear.

"Gentlemen," said the Dexter Lord of Legges, "the question is this: Are the children of disclaiming peers still children of peers; and, if not, whose children are they? Would you like to kick off, Rouge Garter Extraordinary?"

Rouge Garter Extraordinary: Well, let's put this question another way. Can commoners whose children are peers' children be in any meaningful sense fathers?

Morte Puissance: Ex nihilo nihil fit. Vide Tollemache v. Tollemache on the strong presumption of non-paternity in the case of an ox that was cited as putative sire of a pig.

Swart Beast: Could not the difficulty be very easily surmounted by requiring peers renouncing their peerages to disclaim the paternity of their children?

Twicester Herald: Then the wife could apply to the courts for a paternity order made out in the name of the extinguished title.

Rouge Garter Extraordinary: The important thing is that these unfortunate children should not be taken away from their homes and put in orphanages unnecessarily.

Morte Puissance: What we must establish here and now, surely, is whether the son of Lord Home (as then was) is Lord Dunglass (as he now is) or Mr. Douglas-Home junior (as he may well be).

Vray Halidom: Or indeed whether *either* of them is the son of Sir Alec Douglas-Home, or the Earl of Home, or Lord Home, or Lord Hume of Berwick, or Baron Hume of Berwick, or Lord Dunglass, or Baron Douglas of Douglas. As he then was. Or as they then were.

Dexter Lord of Legges: Douglas spelt "Douglas" of Douglas spelt "Douglas"?

Vray Halidom: Precisely so, Legges.

Dexter Lord of Legges: Dashed funny way for a fellow to spell his name.

Swart Beast: Anyway, the permutations are endless.

Rouge Garter Extraordinary: There must be some way of telling. There must be some birthmark or other one of them could produce.

Dexter Lord of Legges: What we must ensure above all is that this unhappy young man is not deprived of someone to call "Father." Or "Lord Father," or "Lord Father of Father," or "Baron Father of Berwick," as the case may be.

Twicester Herald: But my dear Legges, surely Sir Alec, as he now is, could register the titles as a public company—Home, Home, Hume, Hume, Douglas and Dunglass Ltd.—and appoint himself and his son co-directors of it?

Morte Puissance: Would it not be an equally satisfactory solution if the young man's name was spelt "Mr. Douglas-Home" and pronounced "Lord Dunglass"?

Rouge Garter Extraordinary: How about a new title altogether? After all, we must move with the times. I suggest "Lord Dunglass-Home."

Vray Halidom: I like the note of freshness it strikes. And it's obviously an immensely practical little title for running around in. But—well, frankly, it doesn't *speak* to me.

Dexter Lord of Legges: Beast?

Swart Beast: Well, for my money I don't think you can beat "Lord Douglas-Dunglass." There's a tremendously rugged integrity about that title. It's a valid response—a nexus of creative outgoingness—what I might call an essentially dynamic act of awareness. Also the hyphen takes out for cleaning.

Morte Puissance: I'm prepared to go some way with Beast. But when it comes to sheer, solid craftsmanship, give me a good old-fashioned title like "Lord Douglas, or, As You Like It."

Rouge Garter Extraordinary: Preferably pronounced "Lord Dunglass, or, What You Will."

Vray Halidom: Well, I think, you'd have to go a long way to beat Lord Home Number Fifteen, in B Flat Minor.

Swart Beast: Or the sheer sensual awareness of "The Rokeby Douglas."

Morte Puissance: May I put in a word for "On Hearing the First Dunglass of Spring"?

Dexter Lord of Legges: Well, there we were, then. The team can't make up its mind whether former peers' children are peers' children or not. But we're all agreed that a rose by any other name smells just like a rose, a ruse, a rouglas, or a runglass, as the case may be.

Ron Number

Whatever other unseen beings we do or do not believe in, we are all believers in Ron Number. Ron Number is mysterious, unpredictable, unknowable. But undeniably, Ron Number is.

He speaks to us all at one time or another, and when he speaks, there is no denying the call. The telephone rings. "REPugnance 4278," one says. "Oh," replies the voice, "Ron Number." And rings off.

Ron Number never forgets us. He speaks to us on our birthdays; at Candlemas, Martinmas, Lammastide, and Septuagesima. He remembers us on Mondays. He remembers us on Tuesdays. He remembers us on Wednesdays, Thursdays, and Fridays. He does not forget us at the weekend.

He calls us when we least expect it—saving us from the tedium of being asleep at six o'clock in the morning and interrupting our idle reverie as we sit in the lavatory. When one's guests have been warmed with food and wine to the point where they are just beginning to speak openly and directly from the depths of themselves, Ron Number phones. "Oh," he says, "Ron Number." And afterwards nothing is quite the same again.

What is Ron Number trying to tell us? His utterances are oblique and cryptic. I have humbly recorded the ones vouchsafed to me in the Book of Ron Number, which in the Improved Version comes between the Book of Usually Reliable Sources and the Book of Celebrities. Here is a reading from Ron Number, vii 3-10 as a sample:

"And when the bell chymed, he made answer according to

the law and to the usage of his house, saying: 'REPugnance 4278.' And Ron Number spake unto him, saying: 'Oh.' And Ron Number spake further with him saying: 'Ron Number.' And Ron Number here made an end to his speaking.

"And on another occasion Ron Number spake unto him saying: 'Oh. Oh.'

"And at another chyming of the bell Ron Number saith: 'Oh, terribly sorry.'

"And at another: 'Terribly sorry. Frightfully sorry.'

"And at another: 'I wish to speak to Mr. Chatterjee, in the small room on the first floor.'

"And at another: 'Is that REPugnance 4728? That's right —4728. That's what I *said*—4728. Yes, 47 . . .—oh, 4278? Oh. Sorry.'

"And at another Ron Number saith nothing, but silently departed. Yet was he known even by his silence."

A great deal, of course, has been written by commentators attempting to elucidate these utterances. Most commentators have pointed to the remarkable insistence on a sense of grief for transgression. Others have pointed out that the sum of 4278 and 4728 is exactly 9006. Some have seen the mysterious Mr. Chatterjee as a textual corruption of Mt. Chimborazo.

Almost everyone has been struck by the constant repetition of "Oh," or "O." A minority of somewhat eccentric commentators have taken this to be a revelation of the Golden Number, and have attempted to use the figure zero to compute the date of the invention of the telephone. The usual interpretation up to now has been that it stood for Operator, and was intended as giving a metaphorical corporeal identity to Ron Number to make him comprehensible to the human intelligence. But the most modern commentators read the whole phrase as "O Ron Number!" and regard Ron Number as a self-worshipping entity, a sort of abstraction inherent in the telephone system.

One day, almost all of us more or less believe, Ron Number will come in person. He will ring the front-door bell. "Oh, Ron Number," he will say, and stand there mysterious and awful, the miraculous visual equivalent of the universal way he sounds, as he speaks with the tongues of old ladies, wizened Chinamen, fat company directors, and burly West Indians.

Not, of course, that Ron Numberism is entirely undivided in its beliefs. There is, for example, a sect of telephone subscribers in Bexleyheath, the principal tenet of whose creed seems to be that I am an incarnation of the South Eastern Gas Board.

They ring me up and pray to me. "Oh, South Eastern Gas Board?" ask the more agnostic members of the faith, sceptically. "O South Eastern Gas Board!" the true believers proclaim in resounding vocatives.

As an orthodox Ron Numberist I try to put them right. But you can't combat faith with reason, and the really convinced believers go right ahead and pray to me to heal a sick gas water heater, or provide them with a refrigerator, or even sometimes to take from them an old and ailing gas cooker.

Perhaps they are sustained in their faith by a miracle—a time when after earnest prayers had been offered up to REPugnance 4278 a palsied gas water heater suddenly and wonderously filled with gas and blew up, killing seven. Perhaps they have a chapel of their own, and a wise old preacher who tells them that if when they phone REPugnance 4278 they imagine they hear someone denying that REPugnance 4278 is the South Eastern Gas Board it is only a temptation put in their way to test their faith, and that they should strengthen themselves to overcome it by telephoning twice as often. Perhaps they sing simple gas hymns, like:

> *Oh how the weary heart desires*
> *The golden streets, the pearly gate,*
> *The gaseous heaven of the wires—*
> *REPugnance 4278.*

Only, of course, an argument breaks out as to whether the number is 4278 or 4872, and a schism occurs. But the more schisms they have the better; the more combinations of numbers they try the more people to whom they will have to say "Oh, Ron Number." Yes, whatever our beliefs, and whether we know it or not, we are all doing Ron Number's work.

Highest Common Interdenominator

You've said some hard things in your wilder moments about us poor blighters in public relations, Mike (*said Rollo Swavely, the well-known public relations consultant*). No need to look embarrassed about it—I know it was all in fun. And I agree with you entirely. Oh yes, you won't find a more outspoken critic of the public relations industry than myself, I can assure you. More claret?

But the truth is, Mike, some of us aren't quite as black as we're painted. In fact if you look beneath the surface, you'll usually find that your average P.R. johnny is a rather religious sort of bird. I suppose it's natural, really. If you can achieve a pure and burning faith in your client's tinned soup, or whatever it happens to be, you can probably work up a modest faith in something a little higher. You're using the same muscles, as it were.

I mean, take myself. God knows it's not the sort of thing one goes round boasting about, but I don't mind telling you I'm a sidesman at my local church. I'm not claiming to be a better human being than anyone else—God knows, I'm probably *worse*—but I do find that those moments spent in contemplation of things eternal every week, that brief communion with the solid traditions of the past, have always been a great inspiration in my daily P.R. work.

Anyway, a number of us in P.R. who feel the same way have been getting together recently to discuss how we could use the professional skills we possess to witness. No, no, Mike, not to witness anything. Just to witness. It's a technical phrase. Well, we chewed it over and we decided that if ever there was something crying out for a bit of decent public relations it was the current campaign for Church unity. And that's how we came to launch Oecumenical Promotions Limited.

Let me make it clear at once that O.P.L. is an entirely non-profit-making concern. We're giving up our time simply because we have a passionate conviction that just as religion has a place in public relations, so public relations have a place in religion. The message we want to get across is that as Christians we all believe in more or less the same thing, whatever our sect. And by projecting the right sort of images, by creating the right climate of opinion, the differences can be made to seem less rather than more. Simple, isn't it?

If we can get the financial backing, we intend to give it the whole bag of tricks. Delegations of Jehovah's Witnesses shown round Catholic seminaries by carefully briefed guides: intimate little dinner-parties at the House of Commons where Presbyterians, Orthodox Greeks, and Seventh Day Adventists can get together and have a friendly natter about their differences over brandy and cigars; oecumenical features prepared by our staff for the provincial papers; carefully selected oecumenical scoops for the top journalists. We intend to have a duty Press officer standing by at all times to offer guidance on any items of religious news that might cause inter-denominational misunderstanding—Anglicans giving members of the Royal Family a helping hand with their marriage problems, for example, or prominent Catholics advocating a healthy increase in the population of India.

And of course we're building up a comprehensive library of pictures showing Orthodox archimandrites kissing smiling Unitarians, Catholic cardinals patting the heads of C. of E. toddlers (I have one delighful study I've titled: "Non angeli sed anglicani"), and the Archbishop of Canterbury drinking

34

coffee with almost everyone. Oh, just a moment—I'd forgotten about the Mormons. I'd better change all the Canterbury captions to read coffee-substitute.

But all that's just a beginning. What we want to do eventually is to follow the tremendous example set by the Common Market in ironing out local differences. We're going to organise a great drive among the leading European industrialists and armaments manufacturers to raise the funds to build an entirely interdenominational church at Euroville.

Our plans for the Euroglise, as we're calling it, are naturally still tentative. But we envisage a building designed by a committee of leading international architects which is contemporary in tone and yet tactfully recalls all the major trends in European religious architecture. The interior will be equipped with pictorial and sculptural forms by leading abstractionists which can be taken either as Virgins and crucifixes or as purely decorational motifs according to taste. Part of the building will, of course, be set aside for saving a representative international selection of Teddy Boys.

The Euroglise will be staffed by a carefully chosen team of Divine Relations Officers, and the services will be conducted in Basic Eurish. We envisage a simple General Purposes Service, in which a few hymn-tunes would be hummed, an encouraging word or two spoken by one of the D.R.O.s about, say, the preferability of good to evil—without of course being too offensively specific—and a few slides shown of non-controversial missionary work.

Hammering out some generally acceptable form of the Creed gave us a headache or two, I can tell you. All potentially controversial material should be ruthlessly scrapped, we felt. And so we ended up with a very simple and beautiful form of words: just "I believe." That, after all, is what we Christians really have in common; exactly what we believe is clearly of

35

secondary importance. In fact I think there's a good theological case for saying that as with witnessing, what we should aspire to is simply believing, without vulgarising our belief by believing any particular thing. It sometimes tends to sound a bit ridiculous, you know, if you actually specify your beliefs in so many words.

Well, Mike, I know I can rely on your good taste in handling a delicate subject like this. Let me say once again that my colleagues and I are all giving our services absolutely free, and that we've no axe to grind whatsoever. There we are then. And if anyone goes round after this shooting his mouth off about imposing controls on the wicked public relations industry I'll bloody scream.

All the Nudes that's Fit to Print

What influence one's words have! "The Common Market," I said at a dinner given for me the other night, "represents both a challenge and an opportunity." My wife, who was giving me the dinner, agreed entirely. And now Sir William Carr, to judge from a speech he made at another dinner recently, has fallen in with the general lines of my thinking.

This is an important catch, though I say it myself. Sir William is chairman of the *News of the World*—the third generation of Carrs to hold that high office, according to the toast proposed by his editor, and a man with "a great sense of tradition."

With Britain's entry into the Common Market, said Sir William, the newspaper industry would have to ask itself: "Are we alert to all the new possibilities?" He wondered if the industry would be able to meet the new challenge, and declared that success would go to those with new ideas, imagination and energy.

Am I right in taking this as a hint that Sir William is thinking of launching a Common Market edition of the *News of the World*? If he is, I believe we're saved. Our cars may fall to bits; our turnips may be a drug on the market; our bowler-hat industry may lack the necessary crusading spirit; but by heaven, Europe is going to get an almighty shock when the *Nieuws van der Woorld* appears on the scene, done into basic Eurish with a skill that somehow preserves the full fragrance of its chairman's great sense of tradition.

Take this paragraph, picked at random from the dummy I have knocked out as practical evidence of my support:

Ein Matelot, heim von die See ungeexpaektet, squant via ein Keehohl zu giiv die Wief ein wunderlich Surpreis. Bot der Surpreis war der Matelots, und vad e seed via der Keehohl brung Milchdeliveringsman Artur Erbert Botl (42), van Jubileestrasse, Euroville, bevor der Koort dies Week, chaargd mit Oppwicklung, Unpieuwr Schnorring, Grueb, und Beestieheid.

The report, of course, goes into the fullest detail. It tells how after an *Unkorrekt Proposizion* was made in the vestry, *Unkorrektheid* occurred on two occasions at Botl's flat. A girl's clothing had been *Opprompelt*. It was alleged that Botl had been seen *Meddlung mit* in a local lovers' lane.

Under cross-examination, Mrs. X, an attractive young schoolteacher's wife, admitted that *Koziness* had taken place in a tobacconist's shop in Groningen, and again in a dentist's surgery in Oegstgeest. In all, she said, *Koziness* had occurred 19 or 19$\frac{1}{2}$ times.

Detectives kept watch on a laundry for three days, the court was told, during which time 43 *Milchdeliveringsmen* were seen to go in. Police officers who had watched the performance inside 16 times in the course of their duty gave evidence that a girl described as *eine Modell* had held a mousetrap in a *proklaativ* manner. In upstairs rooms they had found *Koziness*, *Unkorrektheid*, *Opprompling*, and *Meddlung mit* going on.

Sentencing Botl to seven years' corrective reading of the *Nieuws van der Woorld*, the judge said that there was no evidence that he had intended to commit *Grueb*, or even *Unpieuwr Schnorring*, but it was the most *Unkorrekt*, *Beestie*, and generally *Kozy kase* of *Oppwicklung* he had ever come across.

"Yes," said Botl later in a commercial on Eurotele, "you

can count me as a fan. I get a real kick out of reading about myself and my fellow *Oppwicklers* and *Meddlers mit* in the *Nieuws van der Woorld*. There's nothing over here that reports our interests and activities so fully and accurately—and with 14 convictions for *Meddlung mit* behind me I speak as something of an expert.

"And I'll tell you another thing. I wouldn't be where I am today if we'd had a Common Market edition of the *Nieuws van der Woorld* when I was a boy. You see, I'm one of those unfortunate people, often referred to by the prosecution in obscenity cases but curiously enough never so far asked to give evidence, who was depraved and corrupted by seeing and hearing certain words.

"It was seeing the Euro-Saxon word '*schn-rt*' written up on a lavatory wall that set me off on the downward road. I repeated it to myself, and after I'd said it once I found myself saying it again—just for kicks, you know. What's the harm, I thought. I can stop whenever I want to. But after I'd said it a few times I began to feel a craving for it. I was hooked.

"Then I felt the need for something stronger. I switched to '*sl-rk*,' and then to '*pr-wt*.' Soon I was mainlining huge doses of the dreaded word '*schm-cker*,' Once I was on to '*schm-cker*,' of course, I was an outcast. My family and friends disowned me. I fell in with a gang of *Milchdeliveringsmen* who went round *Opprompling*, and thought nothing of *Meddlung mit* whenever they got the chance. Finally, *Koziness* occurred.

"If only I had been able to get the *Nieuws van der Woorld* then. If only I had known that '*schn-rt*' meant nothing worse than *Unkorrektheid*! That '*sl-rk*' and '*pr-wt*' were just dear old *Unpieuwr Schnorring* and *Beestieheid*, and that *schm-cker*' was nothing less than the *Koziness* I had enjoyed by my own dear fireside at home!

39

"Yes, as I said at a dinner given the other night by the Benelux Association of Oppwicklers and Meddlers Mit, the *Nieuws van der Woorld* represents both a challenge and an opportunity. Its entry into the Common Market must make us ask ourselves: Are we alert to all the new possibilities? And conversely, I said, in getting the Common Market into the *Nieuws van der Woorld* success will go to those with new ideas, imagination, and energy."

The Patter of Tiny Careers

I was just saying to Lavinia the other evening (*said Christopher Crumble*), sooner or later we've got to decide whether or not it would do us good to have children. Wasn't I, darling?

The point is, of course (said Lavinia Crumble), *whether they'd interfere too much with our careers and our private life. Isn't it, darling?*

. . . I mean, one doesn't want to seem arrogant, but one must face facts. And the fact is, we both happen to have above-average intelligence and taste . . .

. . . *and it would be terribly wrong, we think, not to use them for leading the sort of rich, full lives we're leading now* . . .

. . . because although training a child's mind could in some ways be quite a valuable experience for one . . .

. . . *spending all one's time putting up with a child's tiresome chattering frankly wouldn't exercise the abilities one has* . . .

. . . first and foremost, we both have our careers to think of, don't we, darling?

. . . *and we both find building a career tremendously satisfying and worth-while work* . . .

. . . as you know, Lavinia's just become personal assistant to the deputy head of her department . . .

. . . *and they've practically promised Christopher Bob Pennington's job when Bob moves up to take over from Simon Ward-Turner, haven't they, darling?*

. . . so it would be a wicked waste to do anything that might jeopardise them at this stage . . .

. . . *after all, one does have certain obligations towards one's career, doesn't one?*

. . . and if one can't look after one's career properly one's certainly not a fit person to look after a child . . .

. . . *anyway we find it tremendously satisfying—though of course one needs to get away from it all at times* . . .

. . . which is why travel is so frightfully important. I mean, being so completely without ties we could always throw everything up and go off to the South Seas tomorrow if we felt like it . . .

. . . *only we wouldn't, would we, darling, because of our careers* . . .

. . . then again we think there's a tremendous amount to be said for having children, don't we, darling?

. . . *provided one goes about it sensibly* . . .

. . . because one has to bear in mind that having children does help to broaden one's character . . .

. . . *which is frightfully important, of course* . . .

. . . and make one a more mature and well-rounded human being . . .

. . . *maturity's absolutely vital in a career like Christopher's, isn't it, darling?*

. . . and since we're both earning, we'd be able to afford a full-time nanny and boarding schools, so we should both be able to go on devoting ourselves to our careers . . .

. . . *and travel, if we could find someone to take them off our hands in the holidays* . . .

. . . and still become more mature and fulfilled as human beings . . .

. . . *it makes one think how marvellous it would be if only there were boarding-schools one could send one's parents to as well. We had terrible soul-searchings to decide whether we wanted our parents in our life, didn't we, darling?*

. . . someone really ought to do a study on the pros and cons of having parents, oughtn't they, darling?

. . . I mean, they're sweet to have around at times, but they do make demands on one . . .

. . . for that matter we sometimes think what a shame it is that one can't get a nanny to look after one's friends . . .

. . . I know having friends is terribly important for enriching one's experience . . .

. . . but we find they take up an awful lot of time and attention, don't we, darling?

. . . and it's goodbye to any hope of keeping one's home as one would like it once one has friends coming in and putting lighted cigarettes and wet glasses down everywhere . . .

. . . the truth is that human relationships are expensive luxuries, when you really get down to it, and one has to decide exactly how much they're worth to one . . .

. . . and we do tend to feel that with our careers . . .

. . . and our home, and our travel . . .

. . . and each other, we're really complete in ourselves. Don't we, darling?

England Expects

Daily Pill, Monday:

BINGO'S DAY OF DESTINY

Chris in Row as Clash Looms

Today Bingo will keep a date with destiny.

That is the size of the drama which will be spelled out today during the hectic programme of speculation and forecast on the eve of the Commonwealth Bingo Ministers Conference at Doncaster House.

The substance of today's crucial speculations, I gather, is that tomorrow will be spent largely in the vital eve-of-conference prognostications. I understand that spokesmen expect to be expecting until late tomorrow night.

By Wednesday, when the Conference opens, and Christopher Smoothe, Britain's Minister of Chance and Speculation, hammers home his epoch-making plan for taking Britain into Eurobingo, the key expectations will already be over.

Be ready for a head-on clash between prognostications.

For when Australian Bingo Minister John Trouzies flies into London tomorrow night he is expected to look, in the words of a source close to the official Australian spokesman, "bluff and burly."

I have heard the same words freely applied today to John Holysmoke of New Zealand.

And I predict that tomorrow spokesmen will be expecting Mr. Trouzies and Mr. Holysmoke to line up with bluff, burly John Muffinbaker of Canada.

But I understand that a group of Afro-Asian spokes-men will expect Ngodli Nvectiv of Nghanyika to remain obstinately slim and withdrawn.

FOLLOW THE COMMONWEALTH BINGO
MINISTERS CONFERENCE DAY BY DAY
IN THE "DAILY PILL", THE PAPER THAT
IS ALWAYS A DAY AHEAD

Daily Pill, Tuesday:

WONDERSMOOTHE!

Chris Pulls It Off!

BRILLIANT, MASTERFUL, UNPRECEDENTED.

These were the words astonished spokesmen were using last night to describe Christopher Smoothe's speech to the Commonwealth Bingo Ministers Conference tomorrow.

Amazed Commonwealth Ministers will give Mr. Smoothe round after round of applause. They will clap, stamp, and shout encore, according to one probable eye-witness.

"Nothing like this has even been seen before," I shall hear hard-bitten spokesmen saying in London late tomorrow night.

At one point there will be tears in the eyes of bluff, burly Canadian Bingo Minister John Muffinbaker, it is believed.

In a deliberate attempt to raise the emotional temperature of the conference, Mr. Smoothe will punch home his five-point master-plan for Britain's entry into Eurobingo. This will be a dramatic, unexpected move. Late last night spokesmen for informed sources were still confident that Mr. Smoothe would spell out his proposals rather than punch them home, in a conscious effort to "play it cool."

But make no mistake—yesterday's expectations were only a warm-up. The real test will come today.

Daily Pill, Wednesday:

MUFF LASHES OUT!

Chris in Two-Point Plan Storm

SAVAGELY, RUTHLESSLY, DAMNINGLY.

That is how Mr. Smoothe's critics will slam out at the speech he will make today at the Commonwealth Bingo Ministers Conference. Late last night spokesmen were making no secret of the fact that the speech would be a fiasco.

Mr. Smoothe will sit through the storm tight-lipped and white-faced. Bluff, burly Minister after bluff, burly Minister will condemn Mr. Smoothe's four-point plan to take Britain into Eurobingo.

Even Ngodli Nvectiv, gold-toothed mystery man of Nghanyika politics—welcomed in the past by those close to British spokesmen as slim and withdrawn—will join with Canada's John Muffinbaker today to back a two-point programme of bluffness and burliness.

Mr. Smoothe is expected to console himself for these disastrous forecasts with the knowledge that the real crunch has not yet come. That will be today.

A light rain will be falling as delegates arrive at Doncaster House this morning, according to meteorologists close to the Air Ministry roof. But the colourful traditional robes worn by many of the Afro-Asian Ministers will brighten the scene, I gather.

**(Full text of yesterday's expectations:
Page 6)**

Daily Pill, Thursday:

R-DAY FOR CHRIS

Muff in Air Dash Drama

Today is the vital day of reckoning for Christopher Smoothe's Get-Britain-Into-Eurobingo bid.

For the departure of Commonwealth Ministers from London today after the one-day conference at Doncaster House will touch off a wildfire surge of speculation about what bluff, burly John Muffinbaker and others will tell reporters when they fly in to their home airports.

Yesterday Doncaster House was strangely silent after the drama of expectation and counter-expectation earlier this week. The building was deserted, I understand, except for the Commonwealth Bingo Ministers, who were quietly winding up the week's programme of expectations by holding the Commonwealth Bingo Ministers Conference.

Nothing but a Pack of Ringleaders

I really don't know what some of these lads want (*said Mr. Hobson Nailer, the managing director of Screwe Steel Spoons*). I honestly and truly do not know what some of 'em are after. Seventy-eight unofficial strikes and stoppages we've had in the past year. Seventy-eight! It's almost enough to make me wonder if the company isn't in some way to blame.

Not that we are, of course. No, this firm has a very good record for joint consultation with the union. Spot of bother now and again when we've given some troublemaker the hoof, but we've played fair with them right the way along the line.

Every time we've been forced to lay some of the lads off we've consulted very fully with the union. I'd have the union boys up here myself and put it to them frankly. "We're laying off 35 men in the plating shop," I'd say. "Pick any 35 names you like yourself." If that's not full and frank joint consultation I don't know what is.

Oh, I think the union boys and I understand each other pretty well. They know that if at any time they like to come up here and talk to me their views will always be given a very sympathetic hearing before we go ahead with our plans. What beats me is why the rest of the men won't follow their own leaders. It's the Communists at the back of it, of course. Always stirring it up. And then the rest of them are just like a lot of sheep. Anybody could lead them. Anybody on God's earth.

They've nothing to grumble about here, you know. Some of those lads down there are taking home 30 and 35 quid a week. Well, I say taking it home. Obviously if they're doing that much overtime they wouldn't have a chance to actually go home.

But that's a lot of money. It's almost as much as one of my junior executives gets. And when they break down they can always take a few weeks off on the National Assistance.

Look, it's about 12 o'clock. Why don't we slip across to the directors' dining-room for a quick snort before lunch? I'll show you the executives' lunch-room and the heads of departments' restaurant on the way. We're rather proud of them. Pictures on the wall—waitress service—the lot. Oh, you have to give staff the amenities that go with their status these days if you want to keep them happy.

That? That's the works canteen. We've just had the catering taken over by Industrial Food Handling Ltd. of Walsall, and put in fluorescent lighting and white tiles throughout. Last word in hygiene. Not that these lads appreciate it. Bolt their lunch down and get out again in five minutes flat, some of 'em. Then they go and play football with a tin behind the coke stacks. They're not interested in anything but their pay packets, these boys.

Gin and French? Fine view of the works from this window, isn't it? You see some interesting things from up here in working hours, I can tell you. Look at that laddie there now, reading the paper round behind the washroom where he thinks he can't be seen. It's not the lunch break for another 16 minutes yet, but what does Charlie boy care? By God, I'd like to crack down on some of these lads.

I don't know what some of 'em want, I really don't. All they've got to do is stand by their machines in pleasant workshops—we've just had them all painted green and cream, last word in industrial psychology—pull the lever every time a spoon goes by, and line up for their money at the end of the week. They don't have to think, or take any responsibility, or worry about anything on God's earth.

But do you think they can manage it? All right, there's a decent type of lad who does get quietly on with it. But half of them can't find anything better to occupy their minds than whether the foreman said something rude, or whether Charlie boy on the next machine is going to get his cards on Friday.

I don't know. I had some research laddie down here the other day who said: "Mr. Nailer, don't you think the men would feel they had a greater stake in the firm if they had something of the executive's security of employment and sense of responsibility for himself?"

Well, I told him. "If some of these lads don't buckle down to it," I said, "not even the executive's jobs are going to be safe. Anyway, if they want the privileges that go with the executive's jobs," I said, "let them work for it like I did."

Yes, I've come up from the factory floor myself. I know what it's like—and there were no green and cream walls in my day. I didn't hang around moaning about it. I set to work and got the hell out of it as fast as I could.

There goes the hooter for lunch. Look at them belting across to the canteen. Makes you sick, doesn't it. By God, I'm going to find every last Communist ringleader and troublemaker among them and get my toe behind him, even if it means sacking every spoonmaker in Screwe. In full joint consultation with the union, of course.

Let's go across and have a plate of smoked salmon. I want to introduce you to my deputy, who'll be looking after you this afternoon. No, I'll be off myself—got to take the wife up to town. What you might call an unofficial stoppage! If the Chairman knew I'd get the sack. What? No, just my little joke.

From Each According to His Need . . .

The fog of emotionalism which has always obscured the subject of the Welfare State is lifting at last. After all these years the cold light of reason is beginning to filter through.

The Institute of Economic Affairs has interviewed some 2,000 married men and found that more than half of them—of all classes and politics—thought that individuals should be allowed to contract out of State education, health, and pensions schemes, or that the benefits should be confined to people in need.

This, it seems to me, is plain common sense. Take my case, which I should imagine a great many readers will find typical. I pay £1 a week in national insurance and pension contributions, and a great deal more by way of tax. But during the last 12 months, since I have been neither ill nor out of work, I have not seen a penny in return.

People like us have got the dirty end of the welfare stick. We have to pay contributions like everyone else. But we are too young to draw pensions. We are too healthy to need much medical attention. We have chosen to live in the south of England, and to work in progressive industries like entertainment and property development, where we are unlikely to find ourselves unemployed. Since we work in well-ventilated offices and take care to handle no machine more dangerous than a typewriter or a slide-rule, we are highly unlikely to enjoy any benefits for industrial injury.

Where is our money going, then? Let us not mince words. It is going to support people with incurable diseases, who will be taking money out of the scheme and putting none in for the rest of their lives.

It is going to couldn't-care-less young men who got their hands caught in the conveyor belt, or fell off the scaffolding.

It is being used to finance the birth of illegitimate babies—indeed to encourage illegitimacy by enabling illegitimate babies to get as much orange-juice and cod-liver oil as legitimate ones.

It is buying drinks and cigarettes for unemployed Belfast shipbuilders, who couldn't be bothered to move to London, or to go to the university and train as television personalities. (And remember, men who are unemployed pay nothing at all themselves towards their own unemployment money!)

The truth of the matter is that people fall into two groups whose interests are diametrically opposed, and they are divided in a way that cuts right across their social class and political loyalties. There are the bright, successful, healthy, young people who pay the money in. And there are the slack, unsuccessful, sick, old people who draw it out.

Now those of us who happen to be in the first group have nothing against the others. But if we set all woolly-minded sentiment aside and bring a little cold logic to bear, it is obviously in our interest to contract out of the system and look after ourselves. What we want to see is a system with benefits reserved exclusively for those in need, and therefore, to be fair, paid for exclusively by those in need.

This would have great advantages for all concerned. Our sturdy independence in contracting out would set a fine example to the old, the sick, and the unemployed. It would dissuade us from going off to America to avoid tax, and so depriving the country of our expert knowledge of television and property speculation. It would put money in the pockets of people who would know how to make good use of it—we shouldn't be tempted to waste it, as others might, on the degrading scramble for materialistic luxuries like cars and washing-machines, since we've got them already.

It would make the welfare services more democratic. The two-class welfare system, with a second-class service provided by the State, and a first-class one paid for by the individual, has worked well enough as far as it has gone. But a great many more people could afford the first-class service if they were not also burdened with the costs of the second-class one.

And after all, it's a sensible division of advantages. Since we healthy young people go to the doctor less often than old, sick people, we naturally expect to find on the few visits we do make cleaner, better-decorated waiting-rooms in more desirable houses. For those who are chronically sick it's naturally more of a bread-and-butter occasion, and the sagging canvas chairs and peeling chocolate distemper strike a rather more suitable note.

Then again, the two-class system saves money for everybody. If newspaper editors and Cabinet Ministers had to join the queue for National Health beds, and sent their children to understaffed State schools, they would certainly start insisting on the standards to which they are accustomed. The extra cost would fall on the unsuccessful as well as the successful. The more we can channel off the able and influential people into their own private systems, the more economically we can look after the nobly uncomplaining remainder.

If logic counts for anything, the range of two-class services will have to be extended until all unnecessary contact between the two halves of the nation has been severed. Then, in time, we could move all the Bright people into Southern England, and resettle all the Slack people in the North, where they would have generous reserves set aside for them in the historic Slack homelands, like Tyneside and South Lancashire.

They would, of course, enjoy a considerable measure of tribal self-government in Welfarestan. At any rate, they would be entirely responsible for their own welfare. Seeing that they would all be sick, aged, or out of work, it's a subject in which they should be quite well qualified.

Christmas Ltd.

Christmas means many things to many people (*says a circular I have here from Christmas Ltd., Purveyors of Fine Christmas*). The mounting excitement as the presents are wrapped and the tree decorated . . . the church bells ringing out their glad tidings on a sparkling cold winter morning . . . the happiness of eager children . . . the warmth of the family circle reunited again after the storm-tossed year. . . .

Once again, as we enter upon the genial season of festivity and good will, the familiar expectations are raised. Alas, in how many cases will they be cruelly disappointed?

Long and bitter experience has shown that the idea of Christmas is too precious, too highly charged with nostalgia, too *big* to be successfully realised in practice without expert help. Be honest with yourself—has any Christmas since you were a child ever lived up to your anticipation of it? Haven't circumstances, and human nature, always let you down?

This is where Christmas Ltd. come in. The offer we are making to you is nothing less than this: *we will supply you with Christmas*—a guaranteed Christmassy Christmas containing all the joys you traditionally associate with this glad season and none of the drawbacks! Yes, at prices custom-built to suit the individual pocket, you can leave all the emotional and spiritual overtones of this joyous occasion in the expert hands of our fully Christmas-trained staff!

Here are just a few of the services we offer:

Pre-Christmas Anticipation: Our genial representatives will call in the days leading up to Christmas with generous supplies of fancy wrapping paper, special gift string, Christmas tree decorations, glitter dust, etc., etc. Humming well-known carols, they will fill the whole house up with cheerful and seasonable profusion, leave it at a low rental, and collect it again before it begins to pall.

They will also phone you at times chosen to suit your convenience with remarks like:

"It gets worse every year—the shops are absolutely packed!"

"I've never seen Christmas traffic like it! I don't know why one goes through with it all each year!"

"As if everything else wasn't enough, I hear they're forecasting *snow* now!"

Ambient Temperature Control: As soon as the curtains are drawn on Christmas Eve, you will be astonished and delighted to hear the sound of cars softly crunching over freshly fallen snow outside. Prepaid carol singers will gather at your door with old-fashioned lanterns and the genuine recorded voices of King's College choir, then come stomping into your hall with noses authentically red from the cold, and with *real snow on their boots*!

The Gift Problem Solved: Christmas is a time for giving. But so often the wonderful unselfish pleasure of giving is alloyed by all the trouble involved in finding a suitable gift. Worse, the gift which it did your soul such good to give may be a terrible bore to receive.

Christmas Ltd. have come up with a unique solution. We have evolved a scheme whereby you pay to us however much you feel you want to spend on a present, and we—without extra charge—deliver to the recipient a parcel which contains nothing but your warmest greetings and a quantity of gay, easily disposable gift-wrapping. In this way, your soul is rejoiced without anyone being put under any obligation whatsoever!

(We feel that this scheme will be particularly welcome to the religious, who may well feel that at this season of giving without counting the cost there is something a little inappropriate about expecting anything in return for the money one gives to traders.)

The Spiritual Burden: No need for all those near and dear to you to be in your thoughts at this Christmas season—our fully qualified staff will think about them for you.

No need to worry, either, if you are a little liverish and ill-tempered when the Big Day finally arrives. Christmas Ltd., with their vast organisation, will be feeling quite enough good will to all mankind for your shortfall to be scarcely noticed by mankind at all.

The Human Element: Christmas is traditionally the children's time. It makes everything worth while to see a child's face light up with wonder and excitement at the first sight of the Christmas tree in all its glory, or of the pillow-case full of Christmas Ltd. Gift Scheme gifts that Santa Claus has brought. . . .

Unfortunately, not all children are capable of responding adequately in the somewhat difficult circumstances that often prevail over the Christmastide. They do not believe in Santa Claus . . . they sing improper versions of the carols . . . they squabble over their presents . . . they scream and sulk and cry . . . they are sick on the carpet. . . .

All this is now a thing of the past. We will take any children who cannot really meet the demands of Christmas off your hands and place them in hygienic nurseries for the day. In their place we will supply you with specially selected children who have been trained to believe whatever they are told, with cast-iron stomachs and little faces that light up like search-lights at the sight of anything more remarkable than an old cotton-reel to play with or a bowl of gruel to eat.

On a similar basis, we will also exchange any unsatisfactory relatives left on your hands for replacements guaranteed to emanate self-effacing good cheer and eternal gratitude for all you are doing for them.

And Finally: Our most sincere and heartfelt wishes for a merry Christmas Ltd.!

Behind the Beyond

I think I can take it as generally agreed that every human being has an inalienable right to enjoy a decent inferiority complex, and that, if we are going to have a healthy nation, society must be so arranged that everyone is just behind someone else in the race, to enable us to keep our weight down and maintain our nervous system in high tone.

The point is, which race? I, and a lot of the people I know, keep fit by worrying whether we are falling behind one another in sophistication and worldly wisdom. We each have a secret, nagging fear that everyone else is somehow more *in the know.*

Our conversation is filed down to allusions cryptic to the point of impenetrability. "What Rudolph would undoubtedly call a hundred up," snickers someone, apparently looking at a grapefruit. What? *Rudolph?* Who Rudolph? A hundred up? Up what? Up grapefruit? Up Rudolph? One's mind reels about in a panic, wrestling with formlessness, like a man struggling in the dark with an unidentified something that may turn out to be a burglar, 12 burglars, a gorilla, or a falling coat-stand.

Have I missed something in the papers this morning? Something in the uplifting weeklies? Some delicious scandal everyone else knows about? Is it a subtle jibe at me? Or is it obscene? What disgusting possibilities are opened up by the permutations of Rudolph and the grapefruit? What *not?*

Anyway, one smiles a cryptic, knowing smile. With any luck the smile is as bracing to the other man's nervous system as his remark was to one's own, striking him down with the mortifying conviction that one found his remark painfully obvious, even hackneyed.

And when conversation palls there's always a thrill of tonic anxiety to be had from the uplifting weeklies. The people who write the uplifting weeklies live permanently under the crippling knowledge that by the time they are on sale all the obvious things will have been said already by the uplifting dailies. They'd die rather than be caught saying them again. So they write:

"At the by now famous meeting on Friday of what is coming in certain circles to be known as Mr. Smoothe's Tea-Party, it was not so much what was said as what was not said that was illuminating. Indeed, what one usually fairly vocal member did not say has been significantly played down in Great Smith Street. Nor are there any prizes for guessing who raised a malign eyebrow when a certain party meaningfully quoted Kipling. At any rate, there were plenty of good men and true going round afterwards saying quite openly '1924!'"

It must be people like me who are customers for all those television programmes and uplifting gossip columns that specialise in revealing the inside story, taking one behind the scenes, and getting at what lies behind the headlines.

Take the announcement on Friday by Christopher Smoothe, the Minister of Chance and Speculation, that the Government would build 50 new bingo-halls in the North-East as an emergency relief measure. To born platonists like me such reports are merely the language of appearances, the outer shell of seeming around the inner core of reality, the outside story concealing the inside story within.

The inside men were soon at work on it, revealing that the truth was that on Friday Christopher Smoothe rose at seven o'clock as he always does, drank a glass of orange-juice, then went as usual into the private gymnasium on the top floor of his £50,000 Belgrave Square town house for a 30-minute workout with the roulette wheel. Then down to a traditional breakfast of porridge and devilled kidneys. There was kedgeree on the sideboard, but that morning Mr. Smoothe passed it by.

However busy he may be, they revealed, Mr. Smoothe always makes a point of personally kissing his wife before he leaves for the office. On Friday, since it was fine, he walked to the Ministry, using his own feet. The accompanying photograph shows him striding cheerfully through a typical London crowd of Cockney photographers, colourful reporters, and bowler-hatted public relations men.

This is something like it—the scenes behind the scenes, the headlines behind the headlines. And yet. . . . And yet. . . . Isn't there a story inside the inside story that they're still keeping from us? I mean, can we know the *real* truth about the Government's plan for bingo-halls in the North-East until we know the inside story of the by-now-famous glass of orange-juice? Was it fresh or canned? Did it come from Harrods or Fortnums? Did the by-now-famous Member for West Wittering pour it out for his by-now-famous self?

Still, we're getting somewhere. The cryptic smile I'm smiling now is the inside cryptic smile behind the cryptic smile.

Comedy of Viewers

Thank you, B.B.C. Television! (*runs a letter which Mrs. Ada Vacancy has asked me to use my influence to get published in the "Radio Times."*) What a grand job you're doing bringing culture to people like me! (Perhaps I should explain that though my father was a Featherhead, I am connected on my mother's side with the Easeleigh-Boreables of Bournemouth.)

Your production of *A Comedy of Errors* this week was "just the ticket!" It ran for six-and-a-half minutes by my clock before a single word of Shakespeare was spoken, and my husband and I enjoyed every second.

Of course, all good things must come to an end, and eventually we had to face up to it and suffer "the slings and arrows of outrageous Shakespeare," to coin a phrase! But a word of praise to the actors. Some of their amusing antics between the bouts of literature that followed were highly diverting. They quite "saved" the evening, and as I said to my husband, "They may be 'classical' actors, but some of them are almost good enough for the pantomime in Newcastle!" Which coming from me is praise indeed! (I mean of course Newcastle-under-Lyme, where my mother was born.)

But my "first prize" I reserve for the "back-room boys" who allowed us to see the audience from time to time when things got too bad. There must be many people like myself who now switch on all the cultural programmes on B.B.C. Television in the hope of a glimpse of the audience. I acquired a taste for "audience-viewing" during the lessons which Mr. H. Trevor-Roper gave recently on the subject of (I think)

"History," and I must confess I have become something of an addict!

Of course, addiction to anything can be carried too far! I don't agree with some people who complain bitterly that the "natural breaks" between one picture of the audience and the next are too long. I think these breaks give one a chance to get back to one's ironing!

Perhaps your readers would be interested to know how we arrange our viewing in this house. First we turn the set on in good time for it to warm up before the cultural programme begins. We watch the preliminary antics or trumpet voluntaries—which we love!—and then we turn the sound down. I go out into the kitchen while my husband sits watching the set and listening to the wireless.

As soon as anything of note occurs, he calls me. "Quick!" he says. "Breakdown!" Or it might be someone forgetting his "lines," or even occasionally someone who has had "one over the eight!"

We enjoy all these diversions. But we like the pictures of the audience best of all. They seem such nice, ordinary people —nothing "stuck up" or "special" about them at all. What I particularly appreciate is that they're not fussing about *doing* something all the time, like the majority of the people one sees on the television! Most of the time they're just sitting there quietly, so that one has a chance to take them in and see them as they really are.

Of course, I'm always looking out to see if I can see anyone I know! In one of Mr. H. Trevor-Roper's lessons I saw a young woman who looked exactly like a housemaid I had for a time after the First World War called Susan Hargreaves. I was so surprised that I called out "*Well!* Susan Hargreaves!" My husband dryly pointed out that Susan would be over 60 now!

"It's all right, she couldn't hear me," I said. "The sound's turned down."

How we laughed over that!

Seriously, though, "audience-viewing" does give one a chance to see how ordinary folk can "keep smiling" in the most difficult conditions. A dreary lecture seems to bring out the best in people, just as the war did, and I often hope that some of our national Jeremiahs are looking in, and seeing these wonderful young people doing their best to laugh and keep their chins up. It always brings a lump to my throat.

Alas, there are sometimes one or two "black sheep" in the audience who "let the side down." In that scene in *The Comedy of Errors* in which seven people were sitting in the stalls smiling slightly, with a gentleman on the extreme left who looked exactly like the late Duke of Kent, there was a man in a spotted bow tie who kept laughing in rather a suggestive way. It gave the unfortunate impression that some of Shakespeare's poetry was not so much "immortal" as "immoral"!

I wonder if I might ask your advice in a personal matter? I should like to "break into" television audiences! I am 76, but still young and adventurous in outlook. I realise it is a career which would call for great dedication and a lot of hard work, but I am not quite a beginner—I have nearly 50 years' experience of working in the audiences of various provincial "reps" behind me. I know enough not to expect to star in something like *The Comedy of Errors* overnight!

I should add that my husband has given his blessing to the project.

Your truly, Ada Vacancy (Mrs.)

The Property Speculators

What a lucky old woman I am! (*said Mother*). Having three sons so good to me! You know how much I appreciate your finding the time to take me for a run in the motor like this.

John: You just sit back and enjoy the view, Mother. What do you reckon that one is, then, Ralph?

Ralph: The one with the crazy-paving washdown? Oh, seven, John, at least.

John: Seven? Nine, more likely.

Howard: What about that one there, with all the wrought iron on the sun-lounge?

Ralph: Must be eight or nine, too, Howard.

John: Nearer ten, I'd say. I mean, you know where we are—the Wroxtead Valley estate.

Howard: Oh, it's pricey round here all right. I'm not denying it.

Ralph: Especially up this end. Aren't we just coming out at that five-way junction on the Surley by-pass?

John: That's right. By that new roadhouse there, the Olde Shippe.

Ralph: Hey, look at that one then! With the Jag outside!

John: I'll tell you what, Ralph. I bet that's ten.

Mother: Ten what, dear?

Howard: The HOUSE, Mother. The house is ten.

John: Here's the by-pass, then. Now where?

Ralph: How about cutting down Hatcham Park Road to North Sudstow? We could try out the new underpass in Sudstow Village on the way back.

John: Fair enough.

Mother: Talking about houses reminds me of a house your grandfather's brother Tom once owned. It was somewhere overlooking the river in Chelsea, and Whistler was supposed to have. . . .

John: Yes, but who wants to live in the middle of London, Mother? Pricey round here, you know, Ralph, in Hatcham Park.

Ralph: Pretty pricey.

John: I don't know what one of these houses would cost you.

Howard: Oh, a packet, John, a real packet.

Ralph: I mean, I know a chap in the office—nice chap, got a couple of kids, one of them suffers rather badly from asthma—and his brother-in-law bought, not one of these houses, but one of those big ones up by the cemetery at Upsome. You know where I mean? Well, that cost him close on six thousand, and it wasn't anything like one of these. And that was five years ago, when prices just weren't comparable.

John: I know. I know.

Ralph: What one of these would cost you I don't know.

Mother: Ralph always was the clever one.

Howard: This is more or less North Sudstow here.

John: Not cheap here, you know.

Howard: Quite pricey, by the look of it. What would you say that one with the Spanish-type porch would cost?

John: Must be nine or ten thou. at the very least, mustn't it?

Ralph: What about that new split-level ranch house, then, with the latticed dormer windows? Stop for a moment, John, and let's have a look at it.

Mother: Are we going for a walk?

John: No, no, Mother. Just you sit back and admire the scenery. Shall I tell you what I think, Ralph? This may surprise you, Ralph, but it's really and truly what I think—

Howard: Go on.

John: Fourteen.

Ralph: Fourteen? You may be right at that. I was going to say twelve, twelve and a half.

John: Fourteen. Ah well, let's press on.

Mother: Wouldn't it be nice if one day we could go out into the country on one of these runs? But then I suppose there's no country left these days.

John: Country, Mother? This *is* the country. We're in the Green Belt here.

Howard: Can't you see the grass verges, Mother?

Ralph: Her eyesight's going, you know.

John: Know this road we're joining now? The Vale, Sudstow. You could have got one of these houses here for a song 10 years ago. They couldn't give them away. Now they're six and eight thousand.

Howard: Fantastic, isn't it? Some of these people must have mopped up three or four hundred per cent profit.

Ralph: Does something to you to think about it, doesn't it?

Howard: Beats me the way human beings carry on about things like houses. You'd think they'd have other things to think about.

John: Now I've got a real surprise for you. It's a little road I discovered the other day by pure accident. This next one on the right—Bolderwood Avenue. Take a look at it. They don't make them much pricier than this.

Howard: Very pricey indeed, John.

Ralph: You certainly know how to pick them.

Howard: Look at that one with the weather-boarding on the gables! I should think the garages alone must have cost three thousand!

Ralph: It's marvellous what you can spend, isn't it, when you come down to it?

Howard: What do you think these places would fetch?
   Twenty-five?
Ralph: Thirty.
Howard: Forty, maybe. Fifty.
John: It'd be wrong to guess, Howard. There are some things
   in life you can't reckon in figures alone.
Howard: You're right there.
Ralph: Ah, it's a real tonic just to look at them.
John: Well then, home James?
Mother: It *is* good of you boys to bother with me, taking me
   out to see the world like this. It's a pleasure just to listen
   to you—my word, how you do appreciate everything you
   set your eyes on!

Last Laugh at Marienborn

(The dramatic inside story of the Marienborn crisis, as related by Major-General Sir Roderick Talltrouser, Deputy-Director of Western Face, in a specially written new instalment of his memoirs, "Forty Years of Saving It.")

Marienborn! Throughout the annals of the free world the name will ring like a clarion call. Whenever they hear it, men will lift their heads proudly and say:

"Our tailboards were never lowered!"

Any Communist present will no doubt reply:

"Oh yes they were, so pooh, pooh, pooh!"

Which I'm afraid just goes to show that the Russians are not only totalitarian aggressors, but *bad losers,* and if there is one thing an Englishman cannot stand it is a bad loser.

The truth is that for 41 hours the Americans remained in their lorries on the *autobahn* and valiantly refused all Russian requests for co-operation in counting them. They refused to dismount. They refused to stand up. They refused to lower their tailboards.

As soon as we at Face H.Q. were informed of the Americans' position, we sent out a British and a French convoy as relieving forces, with strict instructions to remain seated and keep their tailboards up at all costs. The Russians, I regret to say, took this as the opportunity to play a particularly dirty trick on the American commander. They told him that at Babelsberg, at the other end of the *autobahn*, the French had in fact lowered their tailboards.

Fortunately, he refused to believe it. "What?" he must

have said to himself. "Is it likely that the French, who did not lower their eagles at Austerlitz or Borodino, have lowered their tailboards at Babelsberg?"

In reality, I am pleased to say, our tailboards held firm all along the line.

The truth of the matter is that the Russians had evidently not bothered to acquaint themselves with the rules by which we play the game—a copy of which we had taken the trouble to forward to them for their enlightenment. In them it is clearly laid down that we will not dismount our troops to be counted if there are fewer than 30 being carried in a convoy, and that in this number we do not include drivers and co-drivers, since they can be seen perfectly well through the windows of the cab without any question of tailboards arising, or indeed falling.

The views of my American and French colleagues and myself, I may say, were in the closest harmony throughout the crisis. At one joint staff meeting the warm emotional tone rose to such a pitch that I became somewhat carried away. I stood up and sang to the assembled Western officers: "British tailboards never, never will be lowered."

At this, I am proud to say, there was applause, and my French colleague jumped up and declared: "*Ils ne baisseront pas!*" The senior American general present added: "Be assured, gentlemen, that when the time comes to stand up and be counted, we will sit down and refuse to be counted." It was a moving moment.

According to our analysis, the greatest danger was the possibility of escalation. That is to say, if we once agreed to lower our tailboards so that our men could be seen and counted, the Russians might immediately go on to insist that they could not really see the men until they had also lowered their trousers.

70

Once this stage had been reached, it was difficult to see how it would be possible to avoid war.

At the height of the crisis we were naturally under pressure from some quarters to offer a compromise. It was suggested that we might provide the shorter Russians present with some sort of box to stand on, so they could see into the lorries, or that we might half lower the tailboards, or that our troops might half stand up with their knees bent.

The waverers were given the short shrift they deserved. I myself reaffirmed our basic beliefs in a very firm memorandum, and I think it might be valuable to recall here exactly what I said.

"Let us make no mistake," I wrote. "Our tailboards are our bulwarks against Communism.

"To be counted sitting down, with the tailboard up, in groups of not more than 30, is one of the basic freedoms that we in the West hold dear.

"Now let there be no misunderstanding about this. To be counted sitting down with the tailboard up in groups of *more* than 30 (not counting those sitting behind glass) is, of course, an entirely different matter. That is not so much liberty as licence, and would not be countenanced by any right-thinking man. We leave such practices to the Communists.

"To put all this in a word—and one which I know our boys out there on the *autobahn* will appreciate hearing—'Tailboards up, chaps!'"

The truth of the matter is this. It has been demonstrated once again for the world to see that the Russians—as anyone who has dealt with them knows—are really just children at heart. To make Ivan lose face is to hit him where it really hurts.

Of course, we should never inflict this terrible retribution unprovoked. But the lesson of Marienborn is once again

71

that our constant readiness to inflict loss of face on friend Ivan is the best deterrent against his doing the same to us.

(*Next week: My secret weapon, the Talltrouser quick-firing Pooh Pooh Pooh gun.*)

OIGMGO

The article in *The Observer* by the Bishop of Woolwich, entitled OUR IMAGE OF GOD MUST GO, and based on his book *Honest to God*, "shall light such a neon sign by God's grace in England as I trust shall never be put out."

Or so the Bishop of Twicester, the well-known progressive divine, will say this afternoon at the mass rally of OIGMGO —the Our Image of God Must Go Movement—in Trafalgar Square. The Bishop will be supported on the platform by some of the most distinguished forward-looking Christians in the country, including Rollo Swavely (the well-known public relations consultant) and Rock Richmond (the eminent teenager).

According to my advance copy, the Bishop will go on to say:

This is a moving moment for me, witnessing at the birth of OIGMGO. As I'm sure some of you know, I have always been a strong supporter of Oecumenical, or broadening, trends in the Church, and opposed to Oiccumenical, or over-demanding ones, and I'm deeply convinced that Oigmgogi-calism is the most Oecumenical and anti-Oiccumenical development yet.

Let's look at this thing in realistic twentieth-century terms. We're in business, after all, like any other enterprise, and one of our directors, the Bishop of Woolwich, has put before us a report telling us why our sales are falling off. He has consulted several go-ahead marketing experts—or theologians, if you wish—and they all say the same thing. God has got the wrong image.

Let's not beat about the bush. If God's got the wrong image, then our advertising is to blame. Some firms benefit from projecting a highly personalised image, by building up the chairman as a lovable human being. Some don't. In spite of all the very lovely material our advertising department has produced on the personal theme in the past, I think we must realise that in the competitive world of today it suffers from a technical drawback which I believe is known in the profession as a low credibility factor. The ordinary man in the street simply doesn't believe it. The Bishop of Woolwich's great breakthrough has been to point out that the ordinary man in the see doesn't believe it either.

Now—if I may keep to the same metaphor—the Bishop of Woolwich didn't just throw in his hand at this point and say that if we couldn't even sell to the staff the firm might as well go into liquidation. As a loyal director his first concern—very properly—is always to find a way of keeping the old firm in business.

So he said: God must have a new image—we must run an entirely new campaign based on the slogan "God is Ultimate Reality." One can only humbly applaud such a masterly grasp of advertising practice. The idea of reality, you see, already has a very high acceptance, and I think people will say to themselves that whatever *Ultimate* Reality is, it is at any rate clearly an *improvement* on reality—a sort of New Wonder Reality containing Formula X.

Then again, it's not offensively specific in a way that might alienate potential customers with preconceived ideas of their own. Nor do I see what evidence the Advertising Inquiry Council could possibly produce to dispute the claim. All in all, it seems to me to be in the same class as "Luxiphags—the Ultimate in Cigarette Luxury."

There's nothing in the new scheme, so far as I can see,

about the Wonderful Free Gift Offer that life subscribers got under the old system. But I'm not sure how much effect on sales it ever had—you did have to save up the coupons for an awfully long time before you saw any return.

And then, as I said before, Square Deal Oigmgogicalism is so wonderfully oecumenical. You can't really be *against* Ultimate Reality, can you, whatever it may be? So in a sense, you see, everybody must be on our side. However, one mustn't fall into the trap of indifferentism, and there is one qualification which the Bishop of Woolwich does lay down. While reality can finally be reduced to mathematical formulae, he says, "what the Christian says is that in, with and under these regularities, and giving ultimate significance to them, is the yet deeper reliability of an utterly personal Love."

Now I don't think we should be too hard on the poor old atheist if he doesn't quite follow us here. I don't want to seem to be casting aspersions on race, colour, or creed, but I rather feel that your average atheist—as charming a fellow as he may be in other respects—simply cannot see how there can be Love in, with, or under anything except in so far as there are beings doing the loving. But then the poor chap probably can't see how there can be Eating without eaters, or Talk without talkers.

Well, we all have our blind spots. *We* can't see how there can be Right without mitres, or Good without gaiters. The blind leading the blind, one might say—but provided it's our lot of blind doing the leading I don't think we need worry too much.

Breakfast Party

(*A daring new experiment in journalism, in which Sir Harold Sidewinder, the well-known chairman and man of opinion, invites Nutria Trousseau, the eminent maritalist, the Rt. Hon. Christopher Smoothe, Minister of Chance and Speculation, and Sir Gwatkin Rockfast, Vice-Chancellor of Twicester University, to join him for a bowl of vintage Rice Krispies, and eavesdrop on themselves as they improvise an entirely unplanned and unscripted column.*)

Sidewinder: . . . to which Lord Curzon replied: "Never, sir."
(*They all chuckle for about three column inches.*)
Smoothe (still chuckling): Yes.
Trousseau (also still chuckling): Yes . . . yes. . . .
Sidewinder: But then, say what you like, the British do have a certain genius for that sort of thing.
Smoothe: Oh, undoubtedly. I speak as someone who has travelled fairly extensively, pretty extensively, in the States, and I can tell you that not once did I . . .
Sidewinder: Oh, there's no doubt about it.
Trousseau: No . . . no . . .
Smoothe: Not *once.* . . .
Rockfast: Oh, it's an art.
Smoothe: Mind you, I think nowadays, if Britain's not to lose her place in an increasingly competitive world, we must keep up with the times. I should like to see a national conference on . . .
Trousseau: That's all you men ever do—talk!
Sidewinder: I take it you believe that should be left to the women, my dear.

76

(*They all chuckle.*)

Sidewinder: What should we do without 'em, bless 'em!

(*They all chivalrously chuckle again.*)

Smoothe: No, but the general principle, surely . . .

Rockfast: As an empiricist, I must admit I tend to be against general principles as . . .

Trousseau: You mean, against the whole idea . . . ?

Rockfast: No, I was going to say that as an empiricist . . .

Smoothe: And who isn't these days?

Sidewinder: I think you've touched on something very important indeed there.

Smoothe: Who can afford not to be an empiricist these days?

Sidewinder: I think you've touched on something very important indeed there, Christopher.

Smoothe: We're all empiricists these days by sheer necessity.

Sidewinder: I think Christopher has touched on something very important indeed here.

Smoothe: I mean, I can remember a time in the thirties—and I don't think I shall be far out if I add *before* the thirties—and for that matter *since* then. In fact I think it was pretty general before the war—and indeed after the war—and of course it exists, it still exists, today.

Sidewinder: Yes . . . yes. . . .

Trousseau: Yes . . . yes . . . yes. . . .

Smoothe: Like the poor, these things are always with us.

Trousseau: Always present.

Smoothe: It's not something you can eradicate overnight.

Trousseau: Here today, gone tomorrow.

Smoothe: Was it Wordsworth who said, the child is father of the man?

Sidewinder: Wordsworth is in a sense a case in point. Wouldn't you agree, Gwatkin? I feel this is more your department, as an Anglo-Saxon scholar. . . .

Rockfast: Well, I was simply going to say that as an empiricist I am opposed to general principles—as a matter of general principle!

(*They all chuckle. Rockfast samples the bouquet of his Rice Krispies.*)

Sidewinder: What do the young think about this sort of thing? In some ways I think, young people today have a very different outlook. . . .

Trousseau: Beatniks. . . .

Smoothe: I saw some young people the other day . . .

Sidewinder: There are a tremendous number of them around these days . . .

Smoothe: They were just walking down the street, as you or I might walk down the street . . .

Trousseau: . . . doing the ton . . .

Smoothe: . . . but I was immensely struck by something in their manner which seemed to cry out: We are not of your generation. We are of our generation. I mean, in a sense, we are not you. You are not us. You are you. We are us. Or perhaps I should say, we are we. I was *immensely* struck by this. *Immensely* struck.

Rockfast: I think everyone must have been struck by this sort of feeling . . .

Trousseau: . . . *tremendously* struck . . .

Sidewinder: Doesn't Cicero somewhere have something . . . ?

Smoothe: I was *very struck indeed* by this . . . by this . . .

Trousseau: . . . by this . . .

Rockfast: Impression?

Trousseau: By this idea, this . . . this . . .

Smoothe: It was very striking indeed.

Rockfast: Yes . . . yes . . .

Trousseau: Yes . . . yes . . . yes . . .

Sidewinder: Yes . . . yes . . . yes . . . yes . . .

(A thoughtful pause. Rockfast sucks reflectively at a fine old vintage pipe.)

Sidewinder: It does reinforce my view that we have a genius for controversy . . .

Smoothe: A talent for constructive . . .

Trousseau: Oh, it is the strong point in the British . . .

Smoothe: . . . for one might say fruitful disagreement . . .

Rockfast: Undoubtedly . . . undoubtedly . . . undoubtedly . . .

Sidewinder: I think it's because whatever other faults we may have . . .

Trousseau: . . . and we do have our faults . . .

Sidewinder: . . . an Englishman is constitutionally incapable of ever being a yes-man.

Rockfast: Yes . . . yes . . .

Smoothe: Yes . . .

Trousseau: Yes . . .

Smoothe: Yes . . . yes . . . yes . . .

(Another thoughtful pause. Smoothe sips a meditative Krispie.)

Sidewinder: You know, I sometimes wonder if that doesn't account for the genius we have in this country for making public entertainment out of private conversation.

Rockfast: First-class entertainment it is, too . . .

Smoothe: Yes, I thoroughly enjoy taking part.

Sidewinder: And one is at one's most . . . one's most . . . one's most *lucid* . . .

Trousseau: . . . to me it always seemed such a *waste* being the interesting, lovable person one was in private if the public couldn't . . .

Rockfast: Yes . . . yes . . . and the most enjoyable moment of all is the one at the end, when they turn the sound down, and leave the faces mouthing silently away behind the credit titles . . . the audience must be afflicted with the most exquisite sense of being excluded from some inmost . . . .

TAKING PART IN BREAKFAST PARTY WERE:

NUTRIA TROUSSEAU, THE RT. HON. CHRISTOPHER
SMOOTHE, SIR GWATKIN ROCKFAST, AND SIR HAROLD
SIDEWINDER.

THE RT. HON. CHRISTOPHER SMOOTHE APPEARED BY
PERMISSION OF THE RT. HON. HAROLD MACMILLAN.

(They all chuckle fine old vintage chuckles in silence for five column inches.)

The Sad Tale of P-t-r B-nnyikin

Once upon a time there was a naughty little rabbit called Peter Bunnykin.

This sentence is almost certainly actionable (noted Mr. K. J. Writweather, barrister-at-law and libel-reader for *Chick's Own*, in the margin of the galley-proof) unless we are absolutely certain that Mr. Bunnykin is no longer alive.

"Naughty" is quite indefensible, and I think to be on the safe side we should also remove the name, since a jury might conceivably hold that calling Mr. Bunnykin "a little rabbit" was damaging.

Even so, Mr. Bunnykin might be able to show that the phrase "a little rabbit" identified him to those who knew him, and I should feel happier if it were removed. If you think "Once upon a time there was," is not strong enough as an opening sentence on its own I should be prepared to accept a completely fictitious description—"a big griffin," say, or "a medium-sized dodo."

Peter Bunnykin lived in a cosy little rabbit-hole in Bluebell Woods.

Any hole in the ground, however innocent it seems, may, unknown to the author, be a Regional Seat of Government, and as such covered by D-notices. I suggest: "He lived in a cosy little dwelling in a wooded location."

One day he decided to go along to Farmer Barleycorn's lettuce-patch and steal a lettuce.

This imputation upon the good faith of Mr. Bunnykin's intentions would be impossible to substantiate. Either "steal" must be changed to "purchase," or else the link with Mr.

Bunnykin must be weakened by changing the sentence to "Later, a rabbit went to Farmer Barleycorn's lettuce-patch, etc." Then if Mr. Bunnykin ever did bring a case I think it could be argued with some success that it was never intended to suggest that the rabbit who took the lettuce was the same rabbit that was mentioned earlier.

Off he went, hippity-hop, hippity-hop.

I suppose this might just pass as fair comment.

With two snip-snaps of his little front teeth he was through the fence around the lettuce-patch.

I suggest: "At another point, a rabbit was in the lettuce-patch." By the sound of it, an action may well lie against the manufacturers of the fencing material, and by the time this story is in print the whole matter may be *sub judice*.

What a bad rabbit he was!

The nearest I can get to preserving the rhythm of this sentence and avoiding any resetting is "What a brown rabbit he was!" I realise this is not very close to the original sense. The best I can do in that direction is "What a broad-minded rabbit he was!"

But he had eaten only two lettuces when Farmer Barleycorn leapt out from behind a hedge and gave him a terrible spanking!

"But only two lettuces had been eaten . . ."—the passive is in general a much less dangerous voice—"But only two lettuces had been eaten when a rabbit and a hand were in collision."

And Farmer Barleycorn said; "It's not the first time I've caught you stealing my lettuces, young Peter Bunnykin."

I think the nearest we can get here, if you are prepared to take a calculated risk, is "Farmer Barleycorn then made a statement."

But coming on top of everything else I'm afraid there is still an element of innuendo even in this. I must admit I should feel safer if it was changed to "Someone said something." Though here again we must ask ourselves, as always, "Will he sue?" I'm afraid that in my experience *someone* always sues. I should sleep easier if we changed it to "No one said something," or better still, "No one said nothing."

Poor Peter Bunnykin slunk off home with his tail between his legs, feeling very small and wishing the earth would swallow him up.

I have as you suggested taken the opinion of leading counsel on this passage, and the more we discussed it, the more ways we could see in which it could be taken to be tendentious. Adding together all our reservations, we suggest: "A certain animal went home in a certain manner, with his tail in a certain position, feeling a certain size, and wishing that a certain object would perform a certain action."

And so Peter Bunnykin lived happily ever after, with a permanent house-guest who was a model with plenty of men-friends: his name connected with members of the Royal Family in vile rumours published by scandal-mongering children's comics on the Continent: being frequently helped home in a state of collapse after gay parties suffering from influenza: with a trunkful of letters from the Under-Secretary for Rabbit Affairs addressing him as "My dear Bunnykin": and described by a Divorce Court judge as a thoroughly rotten, contemptible little rabbit without a single spark of common decency.

This bit seems more or less all right.

Sir,—We are instructed on behalf of our client Mr. Lybell Laws, whose attention has been drawn to an article containing certain extremely damaging innuendoes. . . .

Among the Funny Bones

The evolution of man has not ceased. By the inscrutable processes of natural selection there is evolving from *homo sapiens* a new and more complex species of anthropoid: *homo jocans*, or Joky Man.

Homo sapiens has been defined as a tool-making animal. *Homo jocans* is a gag-making machine. Just as *homo sapiens* became ashamed of his urge to copulate and sublimated it into a culture of solid complexity, so Joky Man has become ashamed of his urge to communicate and is sublimating it into a culture of elaborate facetiousness.

I think Joky Man will prove to be the dominant form. Pre-Joky Man will be made to feel smaller and smaller by Joky Man for failing to see the Joke, until he becomes entirely extinct. By the end of the Uranium Age, Joky Man will cover the whole of the Western Hemisphere. The archaeologists will find his tumuli everywhere, and the remains of Joky Man inside will be instantly identifiable; the skulls will all be trying to keep a straight face.

Our literature does not do justice to the subtlety of our culture. In books people say what they mean, in the antique *sapiens* style. ("Don't you see, Lisbet, that my feeling for Paul is only a desperate counterpoise to Mark's instinctive rejection of Anna?") In life Joky Man speaks almost entirely in irony, sarcasm, understatement, hyperbole, and parody, and I am going to have a fresco painted inside my tomb that will bring home to archaeologists something of the staggering baroque intricacy of life in Joky times.

It will show Joky Man at work, sitting for hours rubbing

gag against gag in the hope of producing a spark. It will show Joky Man at leisure, still chipping one gag against another. A frieze round the margin will display the huge variety of gags a man might have at his disposal—cutting gags, gags that grind the nerves, gags that scrape the bottom of the barrel, gags for falling in love, gags for ending marriages, gags for dying—as well as how a man of small resources might make one or two durable basic gags do for everything.

A further series of panels will show Joky Man speaking in funny voices—joke adenoidal voices, joke television commentator's voices, joke Prime Minister voices, joke Queen voices.

In one of them he will be seen speaking in what he takes to be a joke working-class voice, to show his rejection of bourgeois values and his solidarity with the masses. The panel will include a representative selection of the masses, showing their touching gratitude for this compliment by talking in what they take to be a joke Joky Man's voice.

In a big tableau, Joky Man will be shown speaking in his most important funny voice—what he conceives to be the voice of a low-class theatrical agent. A frieze running round the edge of this scene will make it clear that since he has never actually met a low-class theatrical agent, but only a man whose elder brother's friend does a very amusing imitation of Peter Sellers impersonating Sidney James playing the part of a low-class theatrical agent, this causes no offence to low-class theatrical agents.

The funny-voice series will be surmounted by a tablet depicting Joky Man's larynx, showing typical enlargement and inflammation caused by the strain of speaking with all the voices of men and of angels except one's own. Elsewhere in the fresco there will be scenes from Joky Man's everyday life, with balloons coming out of his mouth reading "Don't call us, we'll call you," "What we in the trwade call a nice bit of crwumpet," "How very different from the home life of our own dear Queen!" "And now—a big hand for someone we all know and love," "My husband and I . . .", "What we in the trwade call one of ourw own dearw queens," "Don't call us, my husband and I will call you . . ."

One whole wall of the tomb will be occupied by a scene representing the spiritual core of Joky Man's life. On one half of the wall—Joky Man appearing on television, saying satirical things in his theatrical agent voice, his Prime Minister voice, and his commentator voice. On the other half of the wall—Joky Man watching the television, mimicking the performers and maintaining a stream of witty observations about them in no less funny voices. The balloons will make it clear that it is the less joky specimens of Joky Man who appear on the screen, and the more joky specimens who watch. Or that at any rate the ones who appear never seem to manage to answer any of those devasting sallies back.

In one corner of the tomb there will be a small picture illustrating a rather sad aspect of Joky Man's life. It will show him trying to say something straight, in his own voice. He is red in the face and glassy-eyed with the effort, but as the archaeologists will see, the balloon that is emerging from his mouth is completely empty. In the last picture Joky Man is being carried off, deceased from an excess of humours. As the headstone movingly records:

"Here lies what we in the trwade call dead funny."

Fog-like Sensations

(According to some sympathisers, the reason why drivers on the motorways failed to slow down in thick fog recently, and so crashed into each other in multiple collisions of up to thirty vehicles, was simply because the authorities had failed to provide illuminated signs explaining that the fog was fog. This is a situation on which Wittgenstein made one or two helpful remarks in a previously unpublished section of "Philosophical Investigations".)

694. Someone says, with every sign of bewilderment (wrinkled forehead, widened eyes, an anxious set to the mouth): "I do not know there is fog on the road unless it is accompanied by an illuminated sign saying 'fog'."

When we hear this, we feel dizzy. We experience the sort of sensations that go with meeting an old friend one believed was dead. I want to say: "But *this* is the man philosophers are always telling us about! This is the man who does not understand—the man who goes on asking for explanations after everything has been explained!"

(A sort of Socratic Oliver Twist. Compare the feelings one would have on meeting Oliver Twist in the flesh. "And now I want you to meet Oliver Twist."—"But . . . !")

695. Now I feel a different sort of excitement. I see in a flash a thought forming as it were before my mind's eye—"This is at last the sort of situation which philosophers have always waited for—the sort of situation in which one as a philosopher can offer practical help!"

696. Imagine that the motorist said: "The trouble is, I can't see the fog for the fog." We might understand this as a

request for *practical* information, and try to answer it by showing him the definition of "fog" in the dictionary. To this he might reply: "I can't see 'fog' for the fog." We respond by putting the dictionary an inch in front of his eyes. Now he says: "I can't see the fog for 'fog'."

697. At this point a philosopher might want to say: "He sees the fog but he does not perceive its fogginess." Ask yourself what could possibly be the object of saying this.

698. Now the man says: "I can see the fog perfectly well, but I don't know that it's fog." I feel an urge to say: "Yet you know it's fog that you don't know to be fog!" (The deceptively normal air of paradoxes.) One can imagine his replying: "Naturally—it looks like fog." Or, if he is familiar with philosophical language: "Of course—I know that I am having fog-like sensations." And if one asked him what he meant by *that*, perhaps he would say: "It looks like what I see in places where I should know what I was seeing if it were labelled 'fog'."

699. *Now* the feeling of dizziness vanishes. We feel we want to say: "Now it seems more like a dull throbbing behind the eyes."

700. Of course, one is familiar with the experience of seeing something ambiguous. "Now it is the Taj Mahal—now it is fog." And one can imagine having a procedural rule that anything ambiguous should be treated as the Taj Mahal unless we see that it is labelled "fog."

701. The motorist replies: "What sort of rule is this? Surely the best guarantee I can have that the fog is fog is if I fail to see the sign saying 'fog' because of the fog."—One can imagine uses for the rule. For example, to lure people to their deaths.

702. Still the man seems uneasy. "To be sure that the fog is fog because it is labelled 'fog', I must first be sure that 'fog'

is 'fog'. Now, supposing, without its being perceptible to the naked eye, the top of the 'o' were slightly open. How am I to be certain that it could not be accepted as a 'u', so that the word was not 'fog' at all but 'fug'? Or how can I be certain that the first letter is really 'f' and not a grossly deformed but still meaningful 'b'?

So now we have to have a label for "fog"! And another label for the label of "fog"!

703. But we are not yet out of the wood! (Or, as one might say, out of the fog.) The motorist might object: "I *still* cannot understand. I see that the fog is labelled 'fog', and that 'fog' is labelled ' "fog" ', and so forth. But how am I to know that 'fog' *means* fog, or that ' "fog" ' *means* 'fog'?

So we must qualify still further. We must expand "fog" to read " 'fog', where 'fog' means fog."

704. Now imagine the motorist's face. Imagine that the doubtful expression remains. Imagine that he says: "But how do I know that the expression " 'fog', where 'fog' means fog" means " 'fog', where 'fog' means fog"?

705. What sort of game are we playing here? What sort of language are we using? I am tempted to ask, what sort of man am I being used by? I have a certain feeling that goes with grating teeth, a frown, flushed cheeks. I want to say: "My offer of help is being abused."

706. One might try to provide the man with a mental picture, a working model of his position—as it were a map to enable him to get his bearings. I might say: "You are in a complete mental fog about the whole business." He seizes on this eagerly. He goes through the motions of assenting—nodding his head, pursing the lips, saying: "Yes, yes, that's it exactly. I am in a complete mental fog."

Now one asks: "But how do you *know* it's a mental fog you're in?"

707. At once he cries: "NOW I see! I see that I don't know I'm in a mental fog at all! I need an illuminated mental sign saying 'mental fog'."

708. If a lion could speak, it would not understand itself.

It

From the Book of It, in the Improved Version:

1. In the beginning, It was.

2. And It was throughout the watches of eternity, yet no man perceived It.

3. And It was revealed unto a certain publicist and sinner, that dwelt among the tribe of Harris-Harris, by the tam-rating trees of Babylon. And his name was Roscoe. He perceived It, that no man had perceived before, and he knew It, and saw that It was good.

4. Then this same Roscoe went up into an high place and lifted up his voice and spake unto Man, saying, Man, get with It.

5. And after he had spoken, there was heard a tinkling as of gold; and after the tinkling there came a rustling like the rustling of banknotes: and after the rustling a great coolness fell upon him. And the people saw that he was with It.

6. And he spake unto Man again, saying, Man, play It cool. And he said, Dig It, Man.

7. And the people hearkened unto him, and got with It, and played It cool, and dug It. And they said, What else shall we do, in order to please It?

8. Roscoe made answer, saying: Have what It taketh. For if ye have, It shall be taken; and if ye have not, even the little which ye have shall be taken also.

9. And he said: Live It up, else shall ye not live It down.

10. And he said, Stay with It. And he said further, Get away from It all. For to be with It wearyeth the flesh and maketh the soul yearn to get away from It all, and to get away from It all is to be with It.

11. And the people wearied of being with It, and got away from It all, and were with It.

12. Now behold, even the scribes and the philistines bow their stiff necks and are with It! Lo, the humble 'ass diggeth It! The great stars of the firmament are with It, and the starlets, the little starlets, partake of the coolness thereof!

13. Some there were among the people that fell down and worshipped Hit. For they said, Hit is the son of It. And whensoever one of their number sang a song, or danced a dance, they fell upon their faces and proclaimed, An Hit, an Hit, an Hit! And they that worshipped Hit were called Hittites.

14. And others there were that puffed themselves up and cried naughtily amid the general worship, Behold, behold, I am not as other men: for lo, I am not with It.

15. But Roscoe forgave them, saying, Verily, ye witness humbly to the existence of It even in boasting that ye are not with It.

16. For this same It is the It of our fathers eternal and ever present. It is the It that is done to do, and the It that is not done to do: It is the It that is written that, and the It that is unwritten: It is the It that is said that, and the It that goeth without saying.

17. For lo, It is everywhere. It is told in Gath. It is published in the streets of Askelon. It is denied in Beer-sheba. It is confirmed by well-informed sources in Gilead. Yea, It is generally known and widely believed.

18. How shall such an One be described? How circumvented? Again I say unto you, Get with It. For It is the Great Passive Principle that underlieth all things.

19. And the people got with It, and great was the profit thereof. And when Roscoe saw that the people had got with It he gave thanks, for he had got away with It. And he lifted up his glass and magnified his salary, saying, Here is to It.

A Species of Evolution

Evolved, that's what he was. Not elected, but *evolved*. It's the new idea. I'm all in favour of it, believe me, since the result has released me from the solemn oath I swore to join the Labour Party if Serjeant Quintin Tread-this-godless-generation-down-in-ammunition-boots was evolved, elected, or otherwise extruded into the form of a Prime Minister.

Yes, I'm a great believer in evolution. I'm not the only one. Every time I've turned the television set on in the past fortnight I've come face to face with some very reliable-looking man who believed in it too.

"It's a question of evolution," each one of them said.

"Through the normal processes of consultation," I would add shrewdly.

"Through the normal processes of consultation," he would go on. "Because, of course, the best way of choosing a leader isn't necessarily just by counting heads."

"Of course not," I'd say. "We have to recognise that some people carry more weight than others."

"I say!" he'd reply. "How jolly nice to find someone who understands!"

"Oh, I heard your friend talking about it last night. We agreed entirely."

"Did you? Yes, well, the point is, of course, that if we just counted heads, the vote of someone who carries a lot of weight, like Alec, or Quintin, or myself, could be completely cancelled out by some ghastly little man no one's ever heard of who might turn out to wear crêpe-soled shoes and say 'bottoms up'."

"How frightful for you!"

"I mean, if it was someone one had been at school with, one could go and talk it over with him sensibly. But a lot of ghastly chaps in R.A.F. blazers—well, I mean to say, one doesn't know them."

"But you take soundings, of course."

"Oh, good heavens, yes! We take *soundings* all right. All the way down to R.A.F. blazer level—and below. Oh, we sound them out all right. Get them on the phone, you know. 'Are you the ghastly little tit who turned up at the Conference in a made-up bow-tie?' we say. 'Well, we're just sounding you out, old chap'."

"And you take note of these soundings, do you?"

"Of course we do. We note down: 'Sounds a decent enough little tit in his way,' or whatever."

"You get right down to grass roots?"

"Exactly."

"But do they carry any weight?"

"The grass roots? Good heavens, yes—they carry the most tremendous amount of weight. Alec, Quintin, and the rest of us walk over them all the time."

"In the Labour Party, of course, they still elect . . ."

"My dear chap, in the Labour Party they simply haven't *heard* of Darwin or evolution. Of course, it's just like the refrigerator or the motor-car—once one's got these things one can't think how one ever did without them. My word, if we'd had to rely on the *election* of species, mankind might never have got where it is today. If every little hog, tick, or sparrow had had his say, instead of soundings being taken among the fellows who really carried some weight, like rhinoceroses and brontosauruses, they might have picked some ghastly little insect as the Lord of Creation."

"I suppose they might. So all this 'election' business is just a lot of antiquated Socialist theorising, is it?"

"Well, what do you think, old chap? You know the slogan—'One man, one vote.' It's the old story of shortages and controls all over again. I mean, I can tell you for a fact that if the Labour Party ever gets into power we're all going to find ourselves issued with ration books allowing us one vote each per election."

"Really? There'll be a black market immediately."

"Of course. Now, our approach is completely different. We say, let any man who has the initiative and the guts to get ahead and make a way for himself in the world increase his voting power as much as he can, and jolly good luck to him."

"That sounds fair enough, I must say."

"Meanwhile, let me assure you, we are sparing no efforts to ease the lot of the old-age pensioners, and increase their voting power to a full ·001 votes per person."

"God bless you for that."

"Naturally, now that the advantages of the evolutionary system have been fully demonstrated, we shall extend them from the party itself to the country at large."

"At the General Election?"

"At the General Evolution."

"Will you be standing yourself?"

"Well, you see, it's not really a question of standing or not standing."

"But you're in the running?"

"I can't really tell you whether I'm in the running or not. It's really simply a question of one's standing in certain quarters."

"One's standing? I thought you said you weren't standing?"

"Oh, quite. But one has a certain standing, you see, notwithstanding whether one's standing or not standing. I mean, where one's lying in the running is simply a matter of certain people's leanings."

"People of standing's leanings?"

"Of course. I need scarcely add, soundings will be taken of the leanings."

"They will? That's all right, then."

"Oh yes—running soundings."

"Running soundings of the people of standing's leanings?"

"Exactly. It's all a matter of evolution."

And More History to Come

Peter Simple, my distinguished counterpart in the *Daily Telegraph*, has hastened to defend our national pageantry against the attack on it made by Philip Toynbee in his review of L. G. Pine's book on the Establishment. I hesitate to jump aboard with *my* views on Mr. Simple's views on Mr. Toynbee's views on Mr. Pine's views on the subject, for fear of bringing the whole human pyramid crashing down among the audience. But I must say that I agree with him. With Mr. Simple, I mean.

As he points out, pageantry is just the collected symbols of history, and if we have more of the stuff than anybody else, it is simply because we have had fewer convulsions to disturb its accretion.

I don't think the pageantry of our national life is dead at all. I believe it is a living, continuing tradition. And provided no convulsions occur, I believe it will go on living and growing, collecting more and more symbols of our history the more history we get to have symbols of. If you think we have enough pageantry already, imagine what a glorious wealth of it we shall have by the time we've got another three or four centuries of our island history behind us.

Take a look at London on a fine summer's day in the year 2362. The centre of the city is packed with Eskimo millionaires and brash Chinese matriarchs queueing to see the sights. There is a queue to buy models of Montgomery's Column in craftsman-chewed chewing-gum. There is a queue to look at an ancient twentieth-century mousetrap, said to be the one that inspired the immortal Agatha Christie. There is a queue to get into the Shell Building, a fine example of the classic commercial architecture of the late 1950s. The Shell Building, of course, has only just been excavated from the dense deposit of crushed steel which completely covered the city during the Great Traffic Jam of London in 1997.

In the streets the rich pageantry of London life has jammed itself to a complete halt. Policemen in traditional period helmets are struggling to sort out the State Opening of the National Economic Development Council from the ceremonial procession to the Royal Variety Performance.

But the two have become inextricably mixed with the cortège bearing the Best Dressed Man of the Year and his fellow clergy to bless Bank Rate at the high altar in the Stock Exchange. And into the middle of this shambles has edged a procession of Hereditary Famous Personalities on its way to take the salute at the Annual Changing of the Christmas Decorations in what used to be Oxford Street.

At this moment there is a blare of martial music, and the First Battalion the Royal Refrigerator Salesmen appear—a brave sight in their traditional grey "jackets" and grey "trousers"—on their way to celebrate Nuffield Day by selling a 21-machine salute of obsolete refrigerators in Hyde Park. Desperately the police divert them up Whitehall—but Whitehall is already full of hired teams of Morris dancers wearing the local costume of striped "trousers" and bowler "hat," and dancing a courtly Sir Roger de Jitterbug to celebrate Sit-Down Day.

Into the middle of this chaos runs the National Dairy Week procession. It is led—for reasons which are lost in the mists of antiquity—by the Chairman of the National Coal Board (a post which is now, of course, a sinecure, apart from the responsibility it carries for censoring all the State collections of pornographic photographs). He bears before him the Golden Milk Bottle, which symbolises a milk bottle, and he is flanked by the Master of the Queen's Advertisements and the Lord Chairman of Amalgamated Spoon Industries, who is also hereditary Chairman of the Governors of the Royal Peeperama House, Covent Garden.

Behind them walk the venerable members of the Ancient Company of Public Relations Consultants, under their motto "Ubique," and the Directors of Unilever, wearing on their colourful traditional ties their proud and ancient coat of arms, which shows a soya bean rampant supported by a sperm-whale in his glory.

And now, in the gilded State Mini-Minor, comes the Queen herself. How entirely radiant she looks, Miss Great Britain 2362! For all her 74 years and her monstrous wart-covered nose, she carries the mind back to those far-off heroic times when the National Beauty Queen was chosen for her beauty, before our more constitutional days when the title passes automatically to the eldest daughter of the Court Engine Driver.

She piles into the great pageant jam. Various members of the Court follow her, until the whole of Central London seems to be ringing with sonorous ancient titles—Miss Fork Lifting Machinery, for example, the *Daily Sketch* Personality Girl, the *Esquire* Book of the Year.

The King of England, a courtier whose title is an even older creation than that of Lord Slough Trading Estate, is casting desperately about to find which procession he is supposed to be attached to, while two of the Court Ushers, the Prime Minister and the Gentleman Editor of *The Times*, struggle after him. The fifteenth Baron Dimbleby, the Lord Commentator in Ordinary, continues to mumble the traditional liturgy to himself, while the 90-year-old forty-third Marquess of Salisbury, the Teenage Satirist Laureate, makes notes for his Official Satire of the proceedings in a complete daze. . . .

Meanwhile, in the great suburb which occupies the whole of the British Isles outside Central London, the rest of the population go through their own humble daily pageantry of collecting symbolic free gift tokens out of surrogate cereal packets to exchange for token free gifts. At last our island history has grown to the point where it fills every square inch of our island geography.

The Ickle World of Stork Shopman

"Dear Mummy," read a communication which fell out as I unwrapped a new cellular blanket for our infant daughter the other day, "My Lan-air-cel blankets are so cuddly and ꝫnugℓly. Get the 'Stork Shopman' to ꝫend Daddy and you a pair and you will sleep so well under your Lan-air-cel I know there ℐℐ are luvly colours for you."

My natural uprush of paternal pride that my daughter should be writing at the age of six weeks was cut short by a handwriting expert, who said the letter was written not by the baby at all, but by the Stork Shopman. I might have guessed. My wife and I have had to read a wide selection of the Stork Shopman's literary production in the past few months, and we ought to have recognised the characteristic tone of diseased fantasy that marks the world of his imagination.

It is a world thickly populated with entities called Bickiepegs, Chu-Chu rusks, Chuckles, and Selflox Todlas. It is a world where everything is decorated with pictures of rabbits wearing waistcoats, and squirrels smirking behind bow-ties. It is also a world whose *materia prima* seems to be a sort of ectoplasm of white, gauzy material, billowing and swirling everywhere uncontrollably like some obscene fog, here gurgling into crocheted trimmings, there snickering and simpering into little bows and frills. I have to hand a picture of a heap of it described as a cot from one of the Stork Shopman's publications, looking like a marijuana vision of the Queen of Sheba's wedding-dress. Against it the Stork Shopman has noted mysteriously: "The most exacting taste could not demand anything more attractive and at the same time more practical. . . . Fully detachable for washing. £23 10s. 0d."

Among the ectoplasm, the anthropomorphic vermin, and the Bickiepegs move an astonishing number of tinplate vehicles, balanced high above the ground on huge wheels like mechanical grasshoppers. Although they are almost entirely identical, the Stork Shopman takes an obsessive interest in differentiating between them. "Pretty Windsmoothe was made to be admired!" he writes about one; "just the pram for the modern mother with streamlined safety in mind!" Or: "Pastorale—the vivacious carriage with the modern family appeal—fun to own, in six dashing colours. Lucky you!"

There is also a character who recurs in the Stork Shopman's works called "Baby." Baby, like Bank Rate, hounds, and God, is a sufficiently important institution to dispense with the definite article. In this state of verbal nudity he peers out from the page swathed in ectoplasm, lapped in a holy glow of muted pastel shades, adored by top models, and hymned with devotional rubrics like "No Jewel More Precious—use lace-trimmed Nappi-pinz to fasten his nappy!" "Only the best will do for Baby—naturally you will want to wash out his spoon in Little Cherub baby-spoon powder."

Do I detect the ugly whiff of heresy here? Is the Stork Shopman trying to persuade us to *worship* Baby? Any day now I expect a complete gospel of the Stork Shopman's heterodox cosmogony to thud through the letter-box, wrapped round a free sample of homogenised groats. In the beginning, he will explain, Baby created the white ectoplasm. And the ectoplasm was without form, and void. And Baby said: Let there be frills and trimmings, and there were frills and trimmings. And Baby called the frills fwills, and the trimmings twimmings.

Baby then makes the Bickiepegs and the Chuckles, followed

by the Nappi-pinz and the Little Cherub. He makes the great perambulators—the Windsmoothe, the Pastorale, the Mayfair, and the Spryte—and orders them to be fruitful and multiply, and cover the face of the ectoplasm.

Then he creates the lesser vermin, dresses them in waistcoats and trousers, and orders them to bring forth abundantly and cover the surface of the great perambulators.

And last of all he makes Stork Shopman in his own image, to have dominion over the ectoplasm, the homogenised groats, the Chuckles, the rabbits, the Windsmoothe, and the top models, and to worship Baby all the days of his life, sounding his praises forth upon a tinkling cash-register. . . .

An unhealthy trend, if I may be forgiven for commenting on a man's sincerely held religious beliefs. And made but little more palatable by the inimitable brand of cuddly, cumfy, ʒnugɛly English in which the Stork Shopman will undoubtedly express it. If he wants my advice, it's to marry a nice girl and raise a family. Once he's got an actual baby on his hands, crying, hiccupping, belching, farting, and drenching all the surrounding napery in its copious humours, I dare say the earthy reality of that flesh-and-blood little animal will put all the old nonsense out of his head. It'll be no loss to anyone. The intellectual daring of the Baby heresy may be ɗugɛ, but frankly the moral tone is merely ʒnugɛ.

Sons and Customers

Chocolates! (*cried Mother*). Well, that *is* kind of you, Ralph. What with flowers from you, John, and bath salts from you, Howard, and you all three driving down to see me like this, I *am* having a lovely birthday! You shouldn't have bothered, you know. I'm sure you've all got much more important things to think about.

Ralph: That's all right, Mother—you only get a birthday once a year, you know. Incidentally, John, do you know where I bought those chocolates? Stanmores in Creese End Broadway.

John: I thought you always bought your sweets and cigarettes in that branch of Goodmans opposite Wemblemore tube station?

Ralph: I used to. But I changed to Stanmores.

Howard: Well, you surprise me, Ralph. I thought you swore by Goodmans.

Ralph: I did. But do you know, I think you get better service at Stanmores. I really do.

John: That's you all over, Ralph—chopping and changing until you find something that really suits you.

Mother: Ralph always was the adventurous one.

John: I admire you for it, Ralph. But I couldn't do it myself. I mean, those flowers—I bought them at Gossards in Broylesden High Street. Now I've been buying flowers at Gossards for 15 years or more.

Ralph: I know you have, John, I know you have.

John: They know me there. They know my name, they know my children's names, they know the sort of flowers I like. Well, they *know* me.

Howard: There is such a thing as loyalty, isn't there, after all? Look at me. I've been taking my car into the Upsome branch of Qualitimotors for 10 years now. They know me. They know the car.

John: You know they care about you. You know you're someone to them.

Howard: I always feel they're genuinely pleased to see me in Qualitimotors. And not just me. They're pleased to see the car.

John: I mean, today for instance. I was going to buy the carnations at 25s a dozen. But the manager said to me, he said: "Frankly, Mr. Tooting, they're not worth it." I mean, he was quite frank with me. "They're not worth the money, Mr. Tooting," he said. "I know you, Mr. Tooting, and if I were you I'd have the chrysanths at half-a-crown each and put the change in my pocket."

Ralph: Oh, I agree. I agree.

John: They know I won't stand any nonsense.

Mother: When it comes to nonsense, a very strange thing happened to me once in a shop in Singapore.

John: Just you sit back and enjoy yourself, Mother. It's your birthday, remember.

Ralph: No, as I was saying, John, I agree with you. Take me now. I get my wines and spirits from a little man in Dorris Hill.

Howard: "Simon the Cellarer" in Manor Park Road, isn't it?

Ralph: That's right. Run by a chap called Nuthall. Been dealing with him for donkey's years now, and when it comes to wines, well, I trust his judgment. "You know, Mr. Tooting," he said to me once, "I never need to ask you—I know it's not the cheap stuff you'll be wanting." Proper character, old Nuthall. And if he gets the orders mixed up he'll always take it back without any argument.

Howard: It's the same with me at Qualitimotors. I always deal with the foreman, of course.

John: Yes, it's the manager who always serves me at Gossards.

Howard: "Hello, Mr. Tooting," he says when I go in. "The old clutch playing up again?" And ready to oblige! Well, I've taken the same repair on the clutch back six times to get it right without anyone saying a word.

John: Mark you, you pay for it.

Ralph: Oh, of course you do. But then you and I expect to pay a bit over the odds. Some people are happy to buy stuff on the cheap, and good luck to them. But you and I have been brought up differently.

Howard: Though it's not just a matter of money, of course. I mean, you go into Qualitimotors in a Jag, flashing a roll of notes, and I don't suppose they'd reckon much to you. But you go in and say I sent you and I think you can be pretty sure they'll look after you all right.

Ralph: If it comes to that, I think you'll find my name's a pretty good passport anywhere along Creese End or Dorris Hill.

Howard: Well, in Higgins and Dickens you've only to mention my name and they'll give you the freedom of the shop.

John: I'm not exaggerating, Howard, but if I so much as raised an eyebrow in Higgins and Dickens they'd get down on their hands and knees and clean my boots.

Ralph: Without a word of a lie, John, I could walk down Creese End Broadway tomorrow and have my boots *licked* clean by the manager of every quality shop in turn.

John: Mark you, I think we've a right to it. I think I can say in all honesty I'm a pretty good customer of Higgins and Dickens.

Howard: Yes, we're all pretty good customers.

Ralph: Well, we all sincerely *try* to be good customers. You can't do more than that, can you?

Mother: Just so long as you try to be good, dear, God will understand.

Shorter Notices

Britain is booming! Or at any rate, emitting a strange, hollow noise not entirely unlike booming. Exports are up, imports are up, the ratio of exports to imports is up, industrial output is up, unemployment is up, and time lost through industrial disputes is up.

There is a lesson for us here. Clearly, the fewer men there are working, and the less time they work, the more they produce. Or, to put it another way, too much output is chasing too little input. Or, as an economist would say, too many cooks spoil the national cake. But then, of course, too many cakes spoil the cook. And too few cakes chasing too few cooks—or indeed even one cake chasing one cook—is something none of us in any party wishes to see happening in this country. It has long been our proud boast that our cooks can go about unarmed.

As a spokesman for National Productivity Year said when he saw the latest figures: "We must tighten our belts to close the gap. Or close the gap up with our national cake. For when the blast of peace blows in our ears, then imitate the action of the tiger. Stiffen the lip, tighten up the gap, and belt the lot up with hard-favoured cake. Up, up, you noble figures! And upon this cake write 'God for NPY, NEDC, and St. NIC!'"

*   *   *

At last! A new political party! How long have you yearned for a thoroughly new party to replace the tired, outmoded parties now in use? How many times have you sighed, "If only they would start a new one. . . ." AND NOW THEY HAVE! We proudly present . . .

THE MODERN LIVING PARTY

. . . as new as tomorrow . . . as British as yesterday . . .

Brought into being in response to overwhelming public demand, the Modern Living Party was founded by the exciting personalities who make up the young-in-heart generation of today . . . Brian Bright, the popular socio-economist and TV personality, Rollo Swavely, the well-known public relations consultant, Cynthia Stocking, former prospective Deb of the Year, Sir Harold Sidewinder, chairman of chairmen and man of opinion, Ken Nocker, the middle-aged teenage satirist . . . to name but a few.

Our slogan GO WITH IT

Our formula for success—The Tories' progressive go-aheadness
—PLUS the Labour Party's respect for tradition.
Our position:

In politics—in commerce—in entertainment—the trend is to the middle of the market. For years all the leading political parties have recognised this—but they have been held back by an outdated fear of extremism, hamstrung by ignorance of precisely where the centre is.

But now scientists at Modern Living headquarters, using all the up-to-the-minute know-how at their command, have located to within tolerances of one-thousandth of an inch our position—*The Extreme Centre*

REMEMBER—WHATEVER IT IS, WE GO WITH IT!

*   *   *

Ivor Newton, who accompanied the late Kirsten Flagstad, has confided to the gossip-columnist of the *Daily Telegraph* that he never heard anything so marvellous as the great Wagnerian prima donna singing the National Anthem as an encore in the Festival Hall. "It was a most thrilling experience," he said.

I am glad that the merits of this lovely piece are at last being recognised. It has, of course, always been a great treasure-house of musical inspiration to English composers. Everyone knows Purcell's elegant set of variations on "God Save the Queen" ("The Queen God Save," "Save God the Queen," "Queen God the Save," etc.), but not everyone has been able to trace its haunting echo throughout the symphonies of Vaughan Williams, and it has only recently been pointed out that the cry of the cuckoo in Delius's "On Hearing the First Cuckoo in Spring" is clearly derived from the setting of the phrase "Our Gra," just before the entry of the second subject, "Cious Queen." Or should I say the second sovereign?

I have made great use of the anthem in the heroic opera cycle I am writing, "The Ring of the Suburbalungen." The theme of the whole cycle is the British people's historic quest through the ages for a worthy national anthem. The haunting "God Save the Queen" theme is used throughout as a *leitmotif* for the hero, Ted, chosen to personify the British people by delegates from both the staff and the employers' sides.

Ted searches the entire kingdom for 100 years—though in the opera-house the period is slightly shortened for production reasons—and eventually, helped by the old English gods Fred and Mucka, finds the words "God Save the Queen" in the mud at the bottom of the Mersey, guarded by three Merseymaidens. When Tee arrives the *leitmotif* sounds, the Merseymaidens automatically stand up, and Ted whips the words from under them.

Over the next 100 years Ted gradually elaborates the magic words until he has:

God save the Queen!
God save the Queen!
God save the Queen!

In the course of the next five operas—each symbolising 100 years of British history and development—Ted discovers the words "gracious," "noble," "victorious," "happy," and "glorious." Finally, in an enchanted castle in the middle of a magic forest, surrounded by gods, trolls, knights-at-arms, Merseymaidens, and flying Valkyrie, he finds the jewelled phrase "Long to reign over us," and he knows at last that this is the best the British people can do.

The opera cycle ends with the famous Prize Anthem octet which, with all eight voices going, sound to the layman roughly like:

"God save long live long live God save our noble gracious happy glorious send her noble save victorious long reign over God save us—the QUEEN!"

Whether the queen is, in fact, saved, my opera does not record.

*   *   *

AN ANNOUNCEMENT FROM THE MODERN LIVING PARTY

The Modern Living Party's direct trading policy:
Other parties are subject to pressures from industry, special interest lobbies, powerful trade unions, etc. By the time these pressures have been passed on to the public via the Conferences, committees, and all the other middlemen of the conventional political party, their effectiveness is inevitably greatly reduced.

Our policy is to let the various pressure groups operate directly on the public without interference.

* * *

April, nature-lovers, is a jolly month for our furry friends the working classes. If you look in the hedgerows now you can see them toiling merrily away again after the long months of doing nothing.

Some well-meaning folk will tell you it is cruel for the little fellows to have nothing to do all winter. Well, you know, it depends. No one wants them to be "unemployed," except where they have become pests and have to be put down. But a great many of the creatures who look "unemployed" are really what we naturalists call *"only seasonally stopped."*

That means it is an entirely natural thing that occurs every winter and there is no need to worry your head about it at all. It can scarcely be cruel if it happens *every* winter, can it, or somebody in this wise old world of ours would surely have put a stop to it long ago.

In fact, I expect some of the little creatures who are used to being "only seasonally stopped" don't much like being back at work again! Perhaps they can cheer themselves up with the thought that if they were only seasonally stopped, they are now only seasonally started.

* * *

Mr. Rollo Swavely, the well-known public relations consultant, wishes it to be known that as a result of his interest in the Modern Living Party, he has of course divested himself of the personal PR account he has hitherto held from the Rt. Hon. Christopher Smoothe, M.P., Minister of Chance and

Speculation. Mr. Smoothe's account has been transferred to a specially constituted firm, R.S. Services Limited. "Naturally," said Mr. Swavely in a statement, "as chairman and managing director of R.S. Services Limited I shall continue to give Mr. Smoothe's account my personal attention."

*   *   *

They don't send us a prize like the National Incomes Commission report every week.

The report demonstrates, with scrupulous fair-mindedness and impregnable intellectual rigour, that the agreements which will raise the average weekly wage of Scottish builders and plumbers (reckoning on a 40-hour week plus eight hours' overtime) from £15 8s. to about £16 10s. are contrary to the national interest.

For proving this, the Chairman of the National Incomes Commission, Her Majesty's trusty and well-beloved Sir Frederick Geoffrey Lawrence, Q.C., is being paid £12,500 a year, and the other two full-time members of the Commission £7,500 and £6,000.

Ah me! The picture of a man being paid £240 a week by the Government to tell another man who gets £15 a week that giving him an extra quid would be a blow at the dear old country's vitals is the sort of thing I lie in the bath for hours dreaming about. That's how I like my humour —laid on with a trowel.

I think there may be more to come. The builders' and plumbers' unsporting refusal to have anything to do with the Commission or its findings should lead the Government to wonder if Sir Geoffrey's £12,500 is not being poured down the drain. Naturally they will set up a meta-commission to investigate, and unless they have abandoned the idea that the appropriate salary of the chairman of an incomes commission is about 15 times the size of the incomes he is investigating, they will have to pay the chairman of the meta-commission a screw of about £187,500.

At that money I'd be prepared to consider having a go myself. In case our trusty and well-beloved Henry Brooke, the Nicholas Luard of the humorous commissions business, is watching, here's a sample of my handiwork:

May it Please Your Majesty, we have examined the agreement by which Your trusty and well-rewarded Sir Geoffrey Lawrence is to receive £12,500 a year in return for attempting to prevent Your average Scottish plumber from being paid more than fifteen pounds a week, and we have come to the following humble and well-excogitated conclusions:

1. Noting the Government's concern to relate wages to output, we have tried to ascertain if Sir Geoffrey's salary can be justified (a) comparatively, by showing that his output is fifteen times as high as that of a Scottish plumber; or (b) expediently, by showing that if he were paid less his output would fall—i.e., that he would not take the trouble to prevent Scottish plumbers from being paid more than, say, seventeen or twenty pounds a week. We found it very difficult to verify either of these hypotheses.

2. We next tried to ascertain if Sir Geoffrey's salary could be justified in terms of the national interest. It seemed to us that logically speaking *all* wages and salaries of any sort are contrary to the interests of everyone but those who are receiving them. Clearly, the less we can get away with paying both Sir Geoffrey and the Scottish plumbers, the more there will be for all the rest of us.

3. To be specific, if Sir Geoffrey selflessly agreed to renounce the price he can command in the open market and to accept whatever valuation we might set upon his services from the

point of view of the national interest, we should be reluctantly forced to advise Your Majesty to pay him nothing at all. (One of the benefits of this would be that Your Majesty would then be better able to afford the £187,500 that *our* trusty and well-upholstered services are setting You back.)

4. Indeed, the only reason we could find for paying anyone anything in a free economy is that he is in a powerful enough position to insist upon it.

5. We feel obliged to report that we can see no arbitrary way of relating wages to national output that any wage-earner in his right mind would accept unless we rearrange our society so that the trusty Sir Geoffrey, the well-advised Scottish plumbers, our good selves, and everyone else, receive approximately equal shares of the national income. However, Your Majesty can scarcely expect someone at present receiving 187,500 crinkly and well-beloved pounds a year to suggest *that*.

*   *   *

AND NOW, A PARTY POLITICAL CHAPTER BY THE MODERN LIVING PARTY

The Modern Living Party's eight-point plan to get Britain on its feet again:

1. DENATIONALISE the honours industry. British earlmakers and knightmakers are second to none in the world. But they are hampered by bumbling State control. They are hamstrung by petty restrictions and favouritism.

Did you know that since the beginning of this year Britain has made only one earldom? Only three baronies and four baronetcies? It is difficult to credit, but not a single dukedom has been launched from a British dukeyard since 1947! And this at a time when the nation is crying out for titles of every description!

2. ESTABLISH each individual rank or order as a public company, to market titles on a strictly competitive basis, without regard to class or position.

3. EXPAND the industry to satisfy the mass market. It is the policy of the Modern Living Party to make this country a titled democracy. A Modern Living Government would offer financial assistance to enable every adult citizen to possess at least one title. Legislation would also be enacted to allow local authorities to acquire titles in bulk and rent them out at cost or below to the less fortunate.

4. FOSTER the growth of the honours accessories industry, from coronets to robes and garters, by constructive legislation on dress.

5. SET UP a Ministry of Honours Planning with wide powers to co-ordinate progress—ensuring, for example, that adequate paper supplies were available to cope with the expansion of 40 or 50 million names, and planning ribbon development.

6. DIRECT the new dukeyards, knighteries, dame works, ermine ranches, etc., into areas where the need for jobs is greatest.

7. SWEEP AWAY vigorously all restrictions at present hindering the development of the export trade in honours. Investigate the possibilities of exporting, under humane conditions, live earls, knights commander, etc. Help the honours accessories industry to break into the international market. We believe Britain has a future as Garter-maker to the World.

8. PROTECT what we hold most dear in our way of life, and ensure that the system of public rewards is not abused, by nationalising The Top. Invest the right to create new personalities in the Sovereign, advised by the Prime Minister and a committee of well-known chairmen and men of opinion. List new creations bi-annually, in the Birthday and New Year Gossip Columns. Exercise the strictest control to prevent the Gossip Columns being touched by the sordid hand of commerce.

*   *   *

Bonanza TV (which serves Bonanzaland from Screwe) has received 945 telephone calls about its production of the outspokenly controversial play "A Midsummer Night's Dream." The Lord Privy Purposes has set up a Royal Commission to help answer the phone.

Viewers heard one character mention the word "bum," and another the word "bloody." Several characters were referred to as "fairies." The play also appeared to condone the use of drugs as aphrodisiacs, and there are expected to be trade union protests about the "undignified light" in which members of some craft unions were portrayed.

Following a threat of legal action, Bonanza broadcast in each interval of the play an assurance that although Flute, the bellows-mender, would undoubtedly call to mind for many viewers Mr. Edward Wrench, the chairman of the well-known firm of Screwe accordion repairers, he was purely fictitious.

Later it was reported that Sir Rufus Bottom was taking legal advice. "I regard the whole play as a calculated slur on my family name," said Sir Rufus. "My father, the late Sir Algernon Bottom, was well known in Screwe. He was a rich mill-owner, and to represent him as a poor weaver is a gratuitious insult to his memory."

It only remains for me to say that I have been asked by Mr. Edward Wrench and Sir Rufus Bottom to make it clear that when I mentioned Mr. Edward Wrench and Sir Rufus Bottom I was not, of course, referring to Mr. Edward Wrench and Sir Rufus Bottom.

Truth is a Many-Splendoured Thing

Through language we subdue the chaos of the universe. Chiefly, I sometimes think, by planting set conventional expressions down among the chaos like fortified towns in a lawless province, so that one can get inside and shut the confusion out. "Unforeseen circumstances," "a prior engagement," "for various reasons"—a sensible man can move from one strongpoint to another without ever getting benighted in between.

As soon as one tries to live outside these safe walls one is fallen upon and annihilated by the forces of anarchy. For instance, you know how it is when. . . . Well, it's difficult to explain exactly what I mean. How can I put it? Look, you know how it is when somebody asks you a question, and the answer seems so complicated that . . .

No, don't go away! Let's try again. What I mean is, sometimes one draws breath to start an exact and truthful explanation of something, when one is suddenly overcome by a vision of the sheer *knobbliness* it's going to involve. The whole thing suddenly seems so maddeningly complex, so knotted with unilluminating conjunctions of trivialities, so beset with irrelevant coincidences that need to be discounted, so dependent on ephemeral minutiae which are meaningless without elaborate glosses, that one's heart fails one, and one lets one's breath out and flees back into the shelter of some less truthful but more manageable explanation.

"How did you come to get that green paint in your hair?" asks someone with no more than a mild passing interest.

"Well," one says, and hoards away two great lungfuls of

air with the intention of laying siege to the truth in some such terms as these:

"This afternoon a man phoned who turned out to be the brother-in-law of a man I once met in New York. Now, this man, the brother-in-law, was staying with a man who had been in college with a man I knew quite well in the Army. Well, this man—the man who had been in college with the man who was putting up the man who was the brother-in-law of the man I met in New York—and whose name, perhaps I should say at this point for ease of reference, is Henry Moore—though not *the* Henry Moore, and no connection with him—though as it happens he *is* a painter (though that's really nothing to do with the matter, except that I don't suppose he would otherwise have had a pot of green paint on top of his bookcase)—anyway this man. . . Oh, I should have explained that there was this *other* man who knew the man who was staying with the man . . . hey, where are you going?"

By the time one's thoughts have foreseen this far, of course, the breath has oozed out of one's lungs and one has mumbled: "I walked under a ladder."

No practical man of affairs ever admits to knobbly explanations for anything. You look at politicians' memoirs. At last, one thinks, when the memoirs of Lord Afterthought, the former Prime Minister, finally appear—the inside story of why we passed the Infectious Aliens (Exclusion) Act and how we came to go to war with Psychomania.

You and I, of course, having knocked around a good deal with some pretty knowing leftist characters in our late adolescence, are well aware that behind the scenes it was the Great Conspiracy at work once again—our old friends Lord Salisbury, Krupp, the United Fruit Company and Geoffrey Dawson, tapping out another nonchalant toccata on the

levers of power. One can hardly expect poor old Afterthought to know as much as that, but it stands to reason he
must have some sort of inside story to tell,

But the inside story so far as Afterthought can remember
it turns out to be that we went to war with Psychomania
because it was high time the Psychomanians were taught a
lesson, and that we passed the Infectious Aliens (Exclusion)
Act because it was felt to be morally incumbent on us as a
Christian nation to see that Infectious Aliens were properly
(Excluded), just like the *Daily Express* said at the time.

If I remember rightly (or rather, if the man I asked about it,
or the man the man I asked asked remembers rightly), Conrad
said that all great events are undertaken in a warm mental
fog. I see his point. But I sometimes wonder. I wonder if
for a moment, before the sheer hopeless knobbliness of it
overcame his strength of purpose, Lord Afterthought almost
dictated to his ghost-writer something more like:

CHAPTER 17

Beneath the Heel of Destiny

The Psychomanian ultimatum was due to expire at
midnight, and just before 11, with heavy heart and
sombre mien, I walked across from my club to Downing
Street to sign H.M. Government's fateful and igno-
minious acceptance.

As I was crossing The Mall I caught sight of a man
who had once been engaged to the sister of a man I had
known well when the man—that is to say, the man
who was engaged to the man's sister—was at school
with another man who later married. . . .

Well, to cut a long story short, I turned sharply on
my heel to speak to him, and the heel came off my shoe.
I could not, I realised in the solemn moment of reflection
that followed, surrender to the Queen's enemies in only

one heel. I therefore determined to advance into Trafalgar Square, repair to the public conveniences there, and reunite the dissident heel to the main body of the shoe by means of a piece of soap.

This manœuvre I executed with some fair measure of success. But it took time, and in my absorption in the Shoe Question I had failed to take into account that the public conveniences in Trafalgar Square are locked up for the night at 11 o'clock. . . .

"I Do Have One Pet Hate," He Laughed.

Great art, I have heard it said, is produced from a fruitful tension between counterpoised forces. So is toothpaste. So is the publicity interview which a man called J. J. Handout is doing with me for an Amalgamated Television press release. In this case the mutually antagonistic forces are J. J. Handout and myself. Unless they're J. J. Handout and the interview form—in which case I must be the one that's being squeezed out. After a few sessions with Handout I feel like extruded toothpaste.

I had a foreboding of what was to come the very first time he rang. "I thought I'd try to knock out a par or two about you, Mr. Frean," he said, and there was a hopelessness about his tone which promised a lifetime shackled together in fruitless mutual torture.

You may wonder why Mr. Handout is interviewing a fellow journalist in the first place. So do I. So, probably, does he. I can only suggest that we are both in the grip of something stronger than ourselves. After all, the interview is the major art form of the era. At one period of history a pair of creative young bloods such as Handout and myself would have inevitably found ourselves writing sonnets. At another we should have been turning out oratorios. But opened out in front of men such as J. J. Handout and myself today is a whole exciting new world of men such as J. J. Handout and myself to be interviewed.

Yes, Sir Harold Sidewinder, J. J. Handout, and all the rest of us in the Communicators' Society will go on interviewing one another until we have tried every possible permutation, or at any rate until we have sucked one another so dry of information and comment that we have reduced ourselves to a fine, exhausted dust, like overworked soil, and been blown away by the wind.

"I don't know whether you've any bright ideas, Mr. Frean?" says Mr. Handout. "I mean, I once did an interview with Rock Richmond, the rock 'n' roll star, all in hip language. You know, real cool, man, and so on. . . . It really brought it to life. I don't know whether you can think of anything along these lines?"

I am forced to admit that I cannot. It's a terrible thing for a young man to have to confess in this second Elizabethan age, but I can't really manage the interview form at all. When I'm doing the interviewing I can never think of any questions, and when I'm the interviewee I can never think of any answers. And I believe future art historians, when they get around to analysing the Golden Age of the Interview, will agree that the purest and most demanding of all the interview forms is the one being attempted here by Handout and Frean—the interview without information content or message, the stark, ultimate, short publicity interview.

Handout and I settle down to work. We start pessimistically enough, but as the shamefully unsurprising facts about my undeviating progress along the standard conveyor belt from birth to early manhood are dragged into the light, it becomes clear that with me Handout has struck a personality as many-faceted and as rich in intriguing odd angles as a billiards ball.

"We couldn't put it that in a sense you were almost sort of expelled from school, could we?" asks Handout desperately. "No? Did you pass your G.C.E., then? Well, perhaps we could put that by saying you were a child genius? Oh, never mind, we'll think of something."

The next time he phones (the relationship between interviewer and interviewee, even for the shortest of short publicity interviews, is a prolonged and intimate one) he reads out the results so far.

" ' "I wouldn't say I was exactly a child genius!" laughed Michael modestly in his West End luxury flat. "But it's not true—as I've heard some people say—that I was expelled from school!" ' It's a line, anyway, Mr. Frean. No . . . No . . I know you didn't actually *say* that, but they like plenty of quotes in these interviews. What do you mean, you don't live in a West End luxury flat? You don't live in a converted manor-house in Bucks, do you? Well, then, take my word for it, you live in a West End luxury flat. Just leave all that sort of thing to me, will you?"

Things go from bad to worse. It emerges that I have no identifiable hobby, no sport, no favourite television performer, no pet animal, no taste for do-it-yourself decorating, no vintage cars, no collection of beer mats or Victorian trombones, no desire to travel, no title. Nor am I related to any member of the aristocracy, leading sportsman, or well known television personality. I am a wash-out. I feel a hopeless sense of profound personal inadequacy.

Things look up for a moment when I remember that I have a wife. But I have to admit that she has no title, either, no hobby, no blood tie with film star or Cabinet Minister. She is not—dare I confess it?—she is not even a top model. Oh God! We have failed as human beings! I keep apologising to Handout, a terrible lump of despair in my throat. It feels just like the day they let me play for the form's second eleven, and I scored two goals against my own side.

"We'll fudge something together somehow," says Handout miserably. "How about some unusual or amusing experience you've had? They usually like something of that sort. ' "Just as the Wrac general inspecting us reached the rank I was in

I heard my braces snap!" laughed Michael. "Was my face red!"' Something along those lines. Or: ' "You should have seen the look on my family's faces when I walked in after they'd got the telegram I'd sent as a joke! They all thought I was dead!"' "

Handout is ringing back tomorrow to find out what I've managed to remember in this price range. How can I tell him that to the best of my recollection I have never had an unusual or amusing experience within the meaning of the phrase? How can I break it to him that I have never seen a ghost, got my head stuck in a pail of whitewash, played a practical joke on my mother-in-law, been mistaken for the gas man, or won a spaghetti-eating competition?

I know he feels I've let him down. He knows I know he feels I've let him down. In fact, we've all the ingredients for a profoundly unhappy relationship as we pan the mud together in the long weeks ahead, searching for some gleam of an unusual hobby, some tiny nugget of amusing experience. "Creative art," said Wordsworth, "demands the service of a mind and heart . . . heroically fashioned." Wordsworth! Thou shouldst be living at this hour! Thou'dst have thy work cut out, I can tell thee.

A Smile a Mile

Mind the Step (*said the Director of the National Safety Slogan Research Laboratory at Screwe*) or You May Mind the Result!

Ah! I see you've hurt yourself quite badly. I'm glad to say "Mind the Step or You May Mind the Result!" was run up in our own laboratories here, so that cry of pain you uttered as you fell was a very encouraging testimony to the accuracy of the work we are turning out.

This is the Production Unit we're in now, where the slogans are actually put together. At the moment I think they're working on "Check Your Tyres—Tyres Get Tired Too!" We've got 30 people here, ranging from Senior Slogan Officers downwards, some of them recruited from university departments—specialists in subjects like Middle English Head-Rhyme, and so on—some of them with years of industrial experience in factories producing Christmas cracker mottoes. As you might imagine, we tend to lose some of our very best men to America—the American humorous greetings card industry is a terrible parasite on British brains and education.

Let's stroll across to my office. Ninety-five per cent of our output is of course devoted to road safety. I may be prejudiced, but I myself think the Government's decision to concentrate the available resources on new slogans instead of new roads was a wise one. If we go on at the present rate, by 1980 we should have a dense wall of sparkling safety aphorism completely filling every gap between Ministry of Transport traffic signs on Britain's major roads.

Here we are, then. Do take a seat. Incidentally, Watch

Out for the Broken Arm—or You May Have One Too! There you go! Broken? No—well, we can't expect a bull's-eye every time.

As you can see, I've had one or two of the slogans we've turned out over the years mounted and hung up around the room. Look at this one—the first slogan to be produced here when we started in 1946: "Keep Left and Be Right!" We've come a long way since then, haven't we? Still, these early models are fascinating to a collector.

Here's a vintage one from 1953—"Think Before You Speed!" It's not easy to get workmanship like that now. I rather like this late 1959 model: "Overtaking is a GRAVE Undertaking!" If you look closely you can see that "GRAVE" is picked out in skeletons and headstones. A rather nice touch, I think.

We try all the new slogans out on our proving-grounds here. They're set up beside the track, and the reactions of our test-drivers are studied and analysed as they drive by at various speeds and in various frames of mind.

There are five drivers in the team, ranging from Very Easily Amused to Totally Humourless, and the job they do is a pretty dangerous one. As a matter of fact, one of our lads was killed only the week before last—our Very Very Easily Amused driver, testing a revolutionary new Manifest Calembour slogan: "Give the Kids a Break (a Brake)!" The film record shows that he doubled up with laughter at Slogan minus five yards. The car went out of control and crashed into "Let them get ACROSS without getting A CROSS!" We shall miss him. They don't make men as easily amused as that any more.

We also test the slogans under actual road conditions. You may have noticed as you drove into Screwe one of our latest ones on trial—"Think—a Moment's Carelessness Could Mean a Lifetime's Carlessness!"—spelled out letter by letter for four miles, just before you get to the municipal sign "Welcome to Screwe—an Accident Black Spot."

Then beyond that we're trying out one of our new Two-Stage Paradox Programmes—one sign saying "DON'T WATCH YOUR SPEED," and then, just as the full impact of that hits you, another one saying "Watch the Road." Get it? As a matter of fact, I think the second one's been knocked down by a lorry, so you may not have noticed it.

We've got some very exciting new projects we're working on at drawing-board level. You did sign the Official Secrets Act on your way in, didn't you? Yes, well, take a look at this:

"Stick to the RULE of the ROAD—Not the ROLE of the RUDE!"

That's the Longslog I, the first of a series of Long Slogans designed to take the driver's eyes off distractions like scenery and girls' legs for several minutes at a time.

Here's something even more up-to-the-minute—the first of a series of design studies done by Ken Nocker, one of the daring new teenage satirists we've just appointed as a consultant:

Have the GUTS
to dip your LIGHTS

Terrifically outspoken, isn't it? When we've got work of this calibre out on the roadside I think we might be able to persuade the Government to branch out into a completely new slogan field—*nuclear* safety slogans, to take the place of all those costly disarmament negotiations. You see, I don't think people realise quite how terrible nuclear weapons are. Do you know that since 1940 *almost as many people* have been killed by nuclear weapons—at Hiroshima and Nagasaki—as we have slaughtered here at home on the roads of Britain?

Dig My Dogma

"If you don't 'dig' dogma," said an advertisement for a religious magazine in *The Times* this week, "you should certainly 'get with' the current issue of *Prism*. The first five contributions concern themselves with John Robinson's 'Honest to God,' and concern themselves with it very deeply. To the agnostic who wrote this advertisement they were intensely stimulating and revealing reading. . . ."

The agnostic whose services were retained by *Prism* to testify to the stimulating qualities of their theology does not reveal his identity. A pity. The astigmatic who wrote this article (his name can be inspected on request at our Erith works) has gone into the advertisement pretty deeply and would have liked to congratulate him on a stimulating and intensely revealing piece of work.

Not to mince words, I thought it was a unique combination of getwithery and godwottery. Or to put it another way, an exquisite blend of dogma and digma. In fact I thought it was the most stimulating and revealing bit of devotional prose published on the subject of John Robinson—known to millions of ordinary religion-lovers as Jack Woolwich—since Mike Canterbury said he was "specially grieved" because Jack had published his views in a newspaper article which was, among other things, "crystal clear in its argument."

Most stimulating and revealing of all was the advertiser's basic idea of getting an agnostic to write the testimonial. It amazes me that Christians didn't think of this earlier. ("To the agnostic who wrote this gospel, the events narrated seem verily 'far out'—but wondrously 'swinging' none the less.")

I hope they will appoint a panel of neutral agnostic advisers to go right through the Thirty-Nine Articles from beginning to end and sort out the stimulating from the unstimulating.

It would certainly be in line with the most enlightened modern practice as I have come to know it. Almost every single article I have ever written on the subject of religious belief has subsequently been either commended or reprinted by some religious publication. I'm not entirely sure with what motive the other cheek is not only turned but so relentlessly hammered against one's fist. But I have an uneasy mental picture of a procession, like the terrible band of medieval flagellants in "The Seventh Seal," crawling across modern England on their knees, grinning with horrible pleasure as they scourge one another with anti-religious satire and blasphemous jokes, bearing aloft images of broad minds, and crying "*Like* us. *Please* like us!"

"May I say how much I'm enjoying this article?" writes the Bishop of Twicester. "I shall certainly take your tip and reprint it, if I may, in my *Diocesan News*, in a section we have entitled 'The Other Chap's Point of View.'

"There's nothing I enjoy more than having my leg pulled— the harder the better! I'm sure God enjoys it, too—though of course the question of whether His Leg exists to be pulled is one which, as you have shown in your amusing articles, we mustn't take for granted too complacently!

"You're absolutely right, of course. We are, alas, sometimes tempted to curry public favour. But it is also true that the best way to protect one's most cherished convictions is not always to stand rigid against the enemy and be cut down, but to smile and co-operate with him. I think some of us are discovering that the Vicar of Bray was not as 'square' as he has sometimes been painted!

"After all, if we go some way to meet you chaps, you can

scarcely help but come some way to meet us! Such is human nature. I saw in the paper the other day David Frost saying that after one of his little religious skits which had offended some people he went to church—and the sidesman told him how much he had enjoyed the programme. One concession calls forth another, you see. I myself had an interesting chat with Ken Nocker after that delightful take-off he did of the Crucifixion, and he told me that it was only the commercial aspects of it he was against really.

"It used to be rock-and-roll singers we found ourselves entirely in agreement with, and then it was teenage satirists. Now it's agnostic copy-writers. Of course, it's a good thing for all of us—it helps to keep our minds open and flexible.

"One of the most encouraging things about the age we live in is this ability not to take ourselves too seriously. There's no harm in behaving like men of the world, after all, and I like to think that we can all enjoy a joke and a prayer together, whichever side of the fence we are on.

"I dare say you'll satirise this letter! It might deserve it, too, for all I know. More power to your elbow—I thoroughly enjoy having my complacency shattered!"

The Mails Must Go Through

Dear Joyce,

Just a line to say thank you for your letter. Lots of news to tell you, but must rush, so excuse scrawl.

I hope you and Howard are keeping well, and that Nicholas and Simonetta are in "rude health." Dominic and Nicolette are both "blooming". They've got through the summer with no coughs or sneezes so far, though I suppose there's plenty of time yet, so we're "keeping our fingers crossed!" John sends his love. Had a letter from Ida on Monday—she and Ralph are both well. She asks to be remembered to you, and says Simon and Nicola are both "blooming." Ralph sends his love.

Well, I must stop rambling on like this or I will go on all night. Must rush to catch the post.

All my love,

Eileen

Dear Eileen,

I expect you will almost faint with surprise to find your ever-loving sister-in-law replying already! Wonders will never cease. The trouble is you're such a virtuous correspondent you make a girl feel the still, small voice pricking away like mad! Wild horses couldn't drag me to take up pen and paper normally, but Duty calls!

Glad to hear Dominic and Nicolette are blossoming. Nicholas and Simonetta are disgustingly healthy, needless to say. Also had a letter from Ida (not usually the world's greatest correspondent, so you see the age of miracles is not past!), and she says Simon and Nicola are flourishing like the proverbial green bay tree. She and Ralph send you their love. Howard sends his love too of course.

133

Forgive the horrible scrawl. Lots more to tell, but must stop now or shall have to go over on to new page, and it's not worth it just for a line or two.

All my love,

Joyce

Dear Joyce,

Just a line to thank you for your letter. Been meaning to write ever since it arrived last Wednesday (first post), but I've been putting it off and putting it off, you know how it is. I feel very guilty for not "doing my duty" more promptly, but I always was a poor correspondent. Somehow I never seem to have the time—I expect you find it much the same. How you manage to keep it up I simply do not know. I suppose some people are just "born" letter-writers! Not me, worse luck, it's a terrible chore.

Dominic and Nicolette are very well—no coughs or sneezes so far, touch wood. Ralph and Ida were over here with Simon and Nicola—all in the "pink." They send their love. How are Nicholas and Simonetta?

Well, I mustn't go on, I'm just indulging myself. I must rush, or you won't get this first post. Please excuse scrawl.

All my love,

Eileen

Dear Eileen,

Don't faint with surprise, but it really is a letter from me. Wonders will never cease. Give a girl the prize. Believe it or not, I feel the stern call of Duty sometimes! I'm quite the little model correspondent—I must be shamed into it by your sterling example! I feel sorry for you having to decipher yet another dollop of my famous horrible scrawl, but on your own head be it—don't say I didn't warn you!

First and foremost, I had a letter from Ida (yes, you did hear right!). Ralph sends his love, and apparently Simon and Nicola

are both A1 at Lloyd's. I trust Dominic and Nicolette are likewise
and ditto. Nicholas and Simonetta I am glad to inform you are their
usual sweet (ha, ha!) selves. Howard sends his love.

Well, the bottom of the page is already raising its ugly head, so I
must restrain what Howard calls my boundless gift for gossip, and
dash to catch the post.

All my love,

Joyce

PS. Must go over on to a new page to tell you—so funny. Had an
extraordinary epistle from Our Mutual Mum-in-law—rambling
on about everything under the sun from French history to politics.
Yes, politics, for heaven's sake, in a letter! I didn't read it all, of
course, but the general gist of it seemed to be that she was well and
sent her love.

Dear Joyce,

Just a line "in haste" to apologise for not writing before, so
excuse the scrawl. Keep promising myself I'll sit down and
write you a really good long letter one of these days, but never
seem to get the chance. You're such a good letter-writer it
makes me feel ashamed of my own poor efforts. I suppose it's
the way you "put" things. I always feel "I wish I'd thought of
that"—but then you've got the gift, haven't you? When I sit
down to write it all flies out of my head. But one of these days
I really will sit down and write you a good long letter.

Well, sorry to have "gone on" so long—I never "know
when to stop," that's my trouble. Must rush to catch post,
so I'm afraid I'll have to close.

All my love,

Eileen

PS. Knew there was something I meant to say—everyone is
well and sends their love.

Oh, Un Peu, Vous Savez, Un Peu

Considering how much at home middle-class intellectuals like you and me feel in the presence of the middle-class intellectuals from the rest of Europe we meet on holiday, it's astonishing how little we can actually communicate. Or, to put it another way, considering the ratio of effort to information in those long holiday sessions of laboured English or paraplegic French, it's amazing we can go on seeing ourselves as having that broad understanding of the world we feel so comfortably in the abstract.

It's different for the spying classes, of course. If the novels do not lie, any plain English spy having difficulties in Bulgaria, say, finds that the smattering of Bulgarian he picked up from collecting stamps as a boy is quite adequate for passing himself off as a used horse dealer from Plovdiv. And when in Chapter 16 he finds himself in the clutches of the notorious Bulgarian police chief, Colonel Khaskovo, communication doesn't falter for an instant.

"So, my friend," says Khaskovo in beautifully starched English, "your foolish inquisitiveness has necessitated our taking certain precautions. It grieves me deeply, believe me, that you will unfortunately not be in a position to appreciate the full fiendish ingenuity with which your so clumsy blunderings will be brought to an end."

How different it all is when the kindly looking lady at the next table in the *pensione*, whom one for some reason takes to be a German, tries to establish some elementary communication by showing a polite interest in one's child. Taking one to be French, she remarks:

"Quel âge?"

In any other circumstances the phrase would be transparently comprehensible. But somehow, spoken in an Italian *pensione* by a woman one takes to be German, a curious obscurity hangs over it. Kellarzh? Kellarzh? Ah, I see—"Qu'elle large!"—obviously Teutonic pidgin French for "How wide she is!"

"Er, ja," one says, tactfully helping the poor soul back to her native language.

"Jahr? Ein Jahr?"

"Ja. Er, ja."

"Ein Jahr! Fantastisch!"

"Oh, *Jahr*. Er, nein Jahr. I mean. . . ."

"*Nine* Jahr? Neun year?"

"Oh, nein, nein!"

"Neun Monat? Neuf mois?"

"Nein nine! I mean, nein neun. Nicht nein—er, neun. Er, excuse me—ich muss à la plage, er, gehen."

Of course, one gets beyond this stage, because the woman and her husband (who are in fact Psychomanian) turn out to speak quite good English. But the further one gets beyond, the heavier the going becomes. For one curious thing, they admire and wish to discuss a whole Pantheon of famous Englishmen of whom one has never oneself heard.

What do we think of Spencer Philips, the philosopher? Oh, really? In their country he is *very* widely read. How privileged we are to belong to the nation that has produced Gordon Roberts, the great modern dramatist, and Philip Gordons, the celebrated novelist. *No?* In their country even the children read translations of them. We shall be saying next that we have never heard of Gordon Spencer, the sociologist, or the world-famous Spencer Roberts, whose political writings have had such an influence on modern Psychomanian thinking!

One tries to return the national compliment, by expressing one's admiration for that grand old man of Psychomanian letters, Sigismund Cortex. Or does one mean Siegfried Catalept? Either way they haven't heard of him.

Worse, whatever level a conversation starts on, it soon comes sprawling down among an unavoidable undergrowth of explanation and counter-explanation. One may start by talking about the ethical well-springs of government, say, but within minutes one is down with one's face in this sort of mud:

"Ah, I must explain. In our country, in each small part of land we have committee governing. What is this called in English?"

"Rural district councils, perhaps?"

"Rura distry council. Yes. In each divided part of land is rura distry council. But in the towns also is rura distry council."

"No, in the towns we call them urban district councils. Or do I mean borough councils?"

"Yes. Of course, the urban distry councils are the underdogs —idiomatic word I learned—the underdogs of the rura distry councils."

"Oh, no."

"In our country oh yes. In our country in the country—can I say that?—is also what you call *country* councils. But I think our country councils are not just the same as your country councils. I must explain. . . ."

I sometimes wonder if Colonel Khaskovo and his friend were correctly reported. What the dreaded Bulgarian police chief really said, I suspect, in the confusion of at last confronting the British master-spy in the secret atomic pile was:

"Mein Gott! Wer ist dies?"

"Wer?" repeats the British master of espionage stupidly, his grasp of German interrogative pronouns slipping somewhat in the stress of the moment. "Dies ist die Pile."

"D. Pile?" repeats the Colonel, momentarily taken aback. "Nicht J. Standish, of British Intelligence?"

"Oh, who, ich?"

"O. Whuish or J. Standish—is no matter. Lay down your arms and put up your arms. Can I say that?"

"Hands."

"Ah, hands, yes. I must explain. I have a firehand here, and if you are not putting up your arms I will pull the—what is in English the little thing hereunder which when one is pulling it makes bang bang . . . ?"

Yes, as our wonderful English poet Markson Spencers said: North is north and south is south: They can only talk with their foot in their mouth.

... To Each According to His Ability

A message from Brian Bright, the popular socio-economist, television personality, and Leader of the Modern Living Party.

Hello out there! It's grand to have this opportunity of meeting you and putting my party's point of view across to you, here in the very centre of the Modern Living heartlands.

You know, more and more people these days are turning to the Modern Living Pary, the new centre party founded with the go-ahead people of today in mind. They're growing weary of the mercenary self-interest of Tories and Socialists alike. And they're getting more than a little sick of the highflown humbug with which both the Tories and the Socialists try to camouflage their purely sectional aims. More and more they want a party which offers them some decent and unselfish *ideals*.

Well, what does the Modern Living Party have to offer? What do we believe in? What are the first principles on which our political philosophy is based?

The answer is simple. Above all else we believe in a fair deal for all. We want to see everyone getting a fair crack of the whip. To put it in a phrase—and it's a phrase which is at the very heart of all our political thinking in the Modern Living Party—we believe in *Equality of Opportunity*.

Now you don't need me to tell you that this country is still the stronghold of privilege—privilege conferred by birth and class. You don't need me to tell you that only too often the real passport to success in this country is not ability, but the old school tie and the right accent. You don't need me to tell you that a man with a title, however dim he may be, can always find a comfortable billet in the boardroom, while others of far greater ability are left outside in the cold.

We in the Modern Living Party are sick and tired of this system. We want to let some fresh air into our hidebound society. We want to see an end, once and for all, to the archaic snobberies that manacle this country and stunt its growth. We want to create the conditions in which everyone has a fair chance to get to the top, regardless of class or accent, regardless of what sort of school he went to, regardless of whether his father is a duke or a dustman.

Now don't misunderstand me. We're not extremists. We're not social theorisers. We don't think everyone's equal meaning everyone's the same. We don't want to mess about with the foundations of society and bring it all down to the same dreary level. We don't subscribe to any high-falutin' theory about paying surgeons the same as roadsweepers.

We believe that men should be equal—*in opportunity*. We believe that they should start level, and that all the doors on the way up should be open to anyone who comes knocking with the right qualifications. We believe that ability, and ability alone, should be the key to the top.

You may hear a lot *talked* about Equality of Opportunity by Conservatives and Socialists. I doubt if you will see much *done* about it by either of those parties. It's obvious why not. The Tory Party draws its principal support from the members of the privileged classes themselves. Do you think they're going to surrender their privileges spontaneously? The Labour Party gets the bulk of its support from the trade unions. Do they show any signs of abandoning the restrictive practices which discount ability by putting the least able worker on an equal footing with the most able?

But now take a look at the Modern Living Party. I think it's fair to say that our membership is typified by the party's National Executive, on which I have the honour to serve. There are people from all walks of life, ranging from Sir Harold Sidewinder, the grand old chairman and man of opinion, to Rollo Swavely, the well-known public relations consultant, and even to Ken Nocker, the teenage satirist and runner-up for TV Personality of the Year.

Most of us are young. Most of us are ordinary—that's to say, middle-class—people. Most of us are working hard at building up careers for ourselves. But we all have one thing in common. The quality we all share (and I say this in all modesty) is *successfulness*.

By that I mean we are the sort of people who are good at passing exams like the 11-plus and the G.C.E., at winning scholarships to the university, at becoming president of the union, and, in general, at doing well for ourselves in a highly competitive world. We are the sort of people who have the ability—provided there are no artificial barriers raised on the grounds of birth or class—to go on rising, right to the very top.

In short, the sort of people who join the Modern Living Party are men and women who enjoy certain natural advantages which they've inherited from their parents, and which they confidently expect to hand on to their children. I make this appeal to you today because I am sure there are many, many people reading this who are of just this type, and who feel in their hearts complete identification with our aspirations and ideals.

To all of you I say this. Come in with us on this great crusade. Turn your back on the vested interests—whether it be the Tory Party's vested interest in the *status quo*, or the Labour Party's vested interest in dragging us all down to the same level. Forget sectional advantage. Let us unite and devote ourselves selflessly to a noble principle—Equality of Opportunity! Remember our slogan: ALL CREAM TO THE A STREAM!

The great explorers of the twentieth century are the journalists; we draw boundaries round previously undifferentiated tracts of the universe and name them. If it weren't for the pioneering endeavours of the Press, some of our most profitable territories, such as the Establishment and the Top, would still be blank spaces on the map.

And with meticulous fairness the newspapers apply the same searching process to themselves. In any newspaper office, a great deal of the available brainpower is devoted to parcelling out the once undifferentiated acres of newsprint in their own publication and subsuming them under permanent general headings—known to the trade as straplines —such as BACKGROUND, BRIEFING, SPOTLIGHT, FOCUS, and DECLARING AN INTEREST.

Every day the papers take themselves further and further to bits and mark each bit with the name of its genus, like an unusually devoted anatomy lecturer amputating his various limbs and organs and pickling them in labelled demonstration bottles. Nowadays papers don't just have articles on corsets and fishing and Mexico; they have features called WITH WOMEN IN MIND, ANGLING ANGLES, and AWAY FROM IT ALL.

It's a very valuable exploration of our own psyche, you see. You lot who merely read the papers may say that if you see an article about corsets you know it's written with women in mind without being told. Well, exactly. Look, do you *like* reading newspapers or something? Well, then. The more words in the paper we can free from meaning, and the more we can fill the old rag up with pointless phrases that stay the same in every issue—the fewer words you actually have to read before you can get on with some more congenial activity.

Anyway, I don't suppose there's anything you or I can do to stop it. Take my word for it, newspapers are going to be broken down more and more into regular named features, until each paragraph has a permanent title of its own. Finally, with any luck, each *sentence* will have its own title, and there won't be any room left for the sentences themselves. You'll all be able to stay in bed for another hour in the morning.

If we're not going to have widespread redundancy in the industry, of course, all the obsolescent reporters and political correspondents will have to be retrained as strapline-writers. It's highly skilled work, and I think somebody ought to be writing a training manual for the course.

For instance, without instruction a beginner might start heading the gossip column GOSSIP COLUMN, and the article on corsets ARTICLE ON CORSETS. For heaven's sake—we might as well all go around stark naked. Or he might start throwing terms such as SPOTLIGHT or FOCUS around when he really meant DAYLIGHT or INSIGHT. There's a world of difference, I can tell you, between spotlighting the new Cabinet, throwing daylight on it, bringing it into focus, and having insight into it. I don't know what the difference is, but then I haven't done the course yet.

And how, without a highly specialised grasp of theoretical biology, can one know what constitutes "living" in such phrases as MODERN LIVING and DESIGN FOR LIVING? Clearly, books, politics and people, are *not*, whereas antique chairs, Finnish glassware, and ducted heating *are*. But what about antique politics, say? What about Finnish glassblowers?

Of course, only experience can teach a man how to pick such titles as IN THE PICTURE and MESSING ABOUT IN BOATS, which have already been matured by use to a smooth finish, and pointless puns, such as JUST YOUR LUCK (for a horoscope), MATTER OF FACT and SPORTING PRINT, which are really part of our great English heritage of punning book and play titles.

Still, I think we could all learn a lot by studying some of the masterpieces of the genre, such as the strapline the *Guardian* puts on Wayland Young's articles, SITTING ON A COLUMN, which makes up for a certain awkwardness by suggesting not one but two unwanted meanings—that Mr. Young is an ascetic, like St. Simeon Stylites, and that, like a chicken, he hatches out his articles by sitting on them.

Anyway, I'd like to retrain as quickly as possible so that I can offer a helping hand to *The Observer*, which still has several pages left without any straplines at all. I'd like to see the news pages entitled THAT WAS THE WAY OF IT, and all the reports of speeches put in a column headed I SAY. We could call the fashion column ARTICLE OF CLOTHING and the car column MOTOR REFLEXES. (Are you starting to feel that delicious dull thud at the base of the skull each time? Think what it will be like when you've seen them all every week for a year.)

MIND OUT OF THE WAY would dispose of the culture pages with a certain sickening finality, and the obituaries would look rather well next to MODERN LIVING in a feature called CURRENT DYING. I don't know about the leaders. VIEWFINDER? OUTBURST? BEEFING? WE CAN'T HELP THINKING?

In the meantime, I'm practising on myself. I call my left hand GRASP, my right foot ON THE RIGHT FOOTING, my eyes DOUBLE EXPOSURE, my backside BASIS FOR LIVING. . . .

Strength Through Joy

What pride of belonging I felt as I stood with thousands upon thousands of my fellow teenage satirists last week at the first Mass Rally of Natsat, the National Satirical Movement! What a sense of comradeship there was in the hall as we listened to the tale of the Movement's triumphs—a West End revue, a revue on Broadway, our own night-club and beer cellar, several newspaper columns, two books, two television programmes, and *Private Eye*, our own party fortnightly!

The rally was held in Backinanger House, Wardour Street, the headquarters of Protest Entertainments Limited, and it attracted delegates from all over the civilised world. Some came from as far afield as Chelsea and South Kensington. So confident was the mood of the rally that it was even generously suggested that an Old Folk's section might be started, where satirists over 25 could spend their declining years giggling over mentions of Lady Docker and Liberace.

The highlight of the rally was the address from our leader, Ken Nocker. The success of the Natsats, he said, was based on their appeal to youth's great reserves of frustrated violence. One of the most satisfactory developments over the past year was the great increase in the movement's scope. "In our early days it might have been thought that we were in favour of some things by default. I think that impression has now been rectified; between us, we are clearly against everything.

"In the past year some potential satirees have thought they could evade their rightful punishment by being failures. We Natsats have changed all that. In the past few months we have not hesitated to ridicule failed playwrights, failed journalists and failed politicians, and to taunt them with their failure in a way that has given pleasure to millions.

"Of course, the fight has not yet been won. Far too much of *Private Eye*, for instance, is still devoted to ends other than wounding. The proportion is decreasing all the time, but the editors should bear in mind that what the public wants is not to be made to laugh or done good to in some nebulous way, but to see people hurt, hurt and hurt again.

"I am delighted to see that in the current issue there is an extended parody of the *Guardian* in which the criticisms of the *Guardian* itself are deliberately stale and second-hand, whereas the innuendoes against individual members of the staff are superbly personal, wounding, and irrelevant to their public functions. That, I think, shows the balance we should aim at.

"We certainly seem to have got the public beaten. A year or two ago, if we had ridiculed a man for being a drunk, or writing a flop, or having a detached retina, all the namby-pamby do-gooders would have whined. But nowadays everybody joins in the fun. Or at least looks the other way. Perhaps they are afraid of being hauled off and satirised themselves as the namby-pamby do-gooders that they are.

"It is strange now to think that our movement started by appealing to men's intelligence and sense of justice to laugh at injustice and stupidity. How limited that appeal was! How much more universal and powerful is our appeal to men's malice, resentment, destructiveness, and envy! And how much more successful we have become since we grasped that truth!"

In the ensuing debate a delegate from the King's Road division called for still sterner measures against satirees. He quoted the maxim: Damage must not only be done but be seen to be done. He called attention to the practice adopted in

That Was The Week of bringing satirees into the studio and insulting them there while their reactions were watched by the cameras.

Could not this idea be more widely adopted? And could not the insults be put on to a more personal level? He would like to see potential satirees such as one-legged public relations men and homosexual Tory M.P.s concentrated in camps for more convenient processing.

Another delegate, from Earl's Court, said that it was good to see some of the old anti-semitic jokes coming back again. Some of his best friends were Jews, and he was sure that they would understand the value of anti-semitic jokes in giving one a valuable feeling of outspokenness after the rather suffocating restrictions of the past 20 years.

A delegate from the Holland Park division proposed that as a mark of the movement's indelible sense of gratitude it should lay wreaths on the tombs of Amis, Wain, and Osborne, the prophets of modern satiricism.

Another delegate said that while he was not for a moment suggesting any parallel between the success of the National Satirical Movement and the spread of the National Socialist Movement (laughter), he wondered if Natsats would not be proud to wear a suitable uniform—perhaps grey denim shirts and elastic-sided jackboots.

Yes, I think we're getting back to the atmosphere of Berlin in the thirties, just like the connoisseurs of those little satirical cabarets have always urged.

Then Come Cuss Me

I sometimes wonder a small, blasphemous wonder. Could there possibly, I think to myself, be any other gods ruling over human affairs? Or is sexuality really the only one?

Now don't misunderstand me. I'm just speculating. Really I'm as devout in my worship as any other member of the Emancipated Church. "O Sex," I pray regularly, just like everyone else, "O wondrous and mysterious Generative Principle, save us all from discontent. Be present in our Koffee-Lux, lest it lose its savour. Manifest thyself in our Mashmaestro electric mixers, that their radiance fall not from them. Betray us not into the hands of loneliness, old age, and thought."

But as a means of universal artistic, spiritual, and intellectual locomotion I'm not sure that it hasn't been somewhat over-driven. I'm beginning to understand how they must have felt about religion by the end of the fourteenth century. How everyone in Florence must have yawned each time the pub-licity executive at the Fourteenth-Century Fox Studios an-nounced that they were painting yet another super-colossal picture with some spurious God-interest grafted on to the plot.

"I know you boys think we ought to make pictures about highbrow subjects like sex," the publicity man would confide to critics over lunch at the Capriccio. "But we have a duty to give the public what they want!

"They don't want to go to the pictures to have a lot of sex rammed down their throats—they've got enough in their lives already. They go to escape from their humdrum sex-bound lives—to identify themselves with some glamorous old saint up there on the canvas as he has fun carrying out feats of single-handed piety and derring-pray in a way for which there's no scope in the hustle and bustle of the fourteenth century. And we do our best to raise the moral tone a bit by slipping in the odd naked woman where no one will notice."

I can imagine what wonderfully snide funny pieces Ken Nocca, the teenage Florentine satirist, used to write about this commercial pandering to the mass audience's lowest common denominator. And how he then went home and got on with the real work which he hoped would justify him as a serious writer—a sensitive novel about a misunderstood young saint on his first year down from the seminary. And I bet he didn't even work any naked women in.

But to get back to this century. I'm inclined to cast around for something entirely new to relieve the monotony. How about resentment? Now there's a powerful instinctual drive even more fundamental to the human condition than sex. Only a proportion of one's relationships have a sexual basis, after all, but is there any human relationship uncoloured by resentment?

I think I'm going to campaign to have the importance of resentment recognised and frankly discussed. Away with this hole-and-corner attitude towards it, this conspiracy of silence. Let us stop resenting shamefacedly and furtively, and resent openly and proudly, secure in the knowledge that it is mutual resentment that more than anything else holds human society together.

I envisage a time when there will be Resentment Guidance Clinics in every town, and when children will be given resentment instruction in school, and not left to find out for themselves in back alleys. Interest will be kept up by conscripting eminent divines to abhor the spread of promiscuous resentment, and to sigh for the days when men and women were too busy with decent healthy lust to have time for all this nonsense.

And I shall be writing my fearless and outspoken novel about Ted and Grace Narkedly, who give hope to millions by coming to the realisation that it is the dark tide of resentment within them that makes life what it is. Here's a banned passage from chapter five, as a foretaste:

"I see the Americans have put another man in space," said Ted. "Lot of bloody warmongers."

"The Prime Minister's called for greater productivity," said Grace.

"Damned old fool."

He looked at her. There was something about her that irritated him dearly. She saw him looking at her, and was irritated by his look. They felt the bond between them.

"Bernard called today," she said. "He's got his fellowship."

She watched the rich thrill of resentment run through him. One's best friend did not get a fellowship every day.

"Really?" said Ted. "I heard that people were saying his wife's going to leave him. It cancels out, I suppose."

He got up sharply, and cracked his head against a beam. Somehow it reminded him of how much there was to resent. He resented his employers' authority over him, he mused. He resented his subordinates' resentment. He resented paying tax.

Outside the window a cold, dirty rain was falling. What a wonderful night it was for resentment! Yes, he realised in a sort of ecstasy, he resented his friends. He resented his relatives. And his friends and relatives resented him. His relatives resented his friends. His friends resented his relatives.

He resented his wife. He resented the Government. The Government resented his wife. . . .

How rich the world was in resentment! For a moment he had a brilliantly clear vision of the universe as a network of interlocking resentments. Everyone resented everyone. Even the beam, he saw with a strange clarity, must resent his head, and his head the beam.

He looked at his wife with new eyes, and gazed for a long time.

"For God's sake put some stockings on," he said at last.

Only resent, he thought. If we didn't resent, some of us wouldn't know we were alive.

(Next instalment: Grace falls in resentment with Bernard!)

At the Sign of the Rupture Belt

There's the shop with the rupture belt outside! (*said Nicolette*).
Now we've driven halfway to Granny's, haven't we, Daddy?

Father: Halfway exactly.

Nicolette: I always remember we're halfway when we get to
the shop with the rupture belt outside, don't I, Daddy?

Dominic: And I always remember we're three-quarters way
when we get to Acme Motors, don't I, Daddy?

Mother: I wish you two would stop your silly pestering. I
don't know why we bring you out in the car to Granny's.

Father: It's good for them to travel, Eileen. They see new
things. They get something fresh to talk about.

Dominic: There's the factory with the rusty bike on the roof!

Nicolette: There's the advertisement for Viriloids Rejuvenating
Pills!

Dominic: There's the Tigers!

Mother: The *what?*

Dominic: The Tigers! That's what we always call the Lyons
there, don't we, Daddy?

Father: We certainly do, son. And there's the brewery where
they brew the Adam's ale.

Nicolette: Daddy always says that now when we pass the
Wemblemore waterworks, doesn't he, Dominic? He
never used to, did he?

Father: What's this place on the right, children?

Dominic: I know! I know! It's the site for the new eye
hospital.

Nicolette: Say your joke, Daddy, say your joke!

Father: It's a proper site for sore eyes.

Nicolette: Did you hear Daddy say his joke, Mummy?

Mother: Are we in Sudstow yet, John?

Dominic: Mummy, you *never* know where this is. You always ask Daddy if we're in Sudstow when we get to the site for sore eyes.

Father: Where are we then, Mr. Knowall?

Dominic: We're just coming to the place where we saw the drunk men fighting——

Nicolette: ——where Daddy always says: "Can you imagine a more godforsaken hole than this?"

Dominic: And Mummy says she can't.

Father: We're just coming into Surley, Eileen.

Dominic: And you're not sure, are you, Daddy, but you think Wemblemore ends and Surley begins just after Wile-U-Wate Footwear Repairs, don't you?

Father: Look at it, Eileen. Scruffy people, cheapjack stores, rundown cinemas. I wonder how many pubs there are in this street alone?

Dominic: There are nine, Daddy.

Nicolette: We always count them for you.

Father: Can you imagine a more godforsaken hole?

Nicolette: Daddy said it, Dominic.

Dominic: Now say you can't, Mummy.

Mother: Oh, do stop pestering. Can't you think of some game to play as we go along?

Dominic: We *are* playing a game, Mummy. But you're not playing it properly.

Nicolette: You haven't said you can't imagine such a god-forsaken hole, has she, Dominic?

Mother: Those children! They're enough to try the patience of a saint!

Father: There's Acme Motors, anyway—we're three-quarters of the way there now.

Dominic: Daddy! That's what *I* say! *I'm* the one who sees Acme Motors and says we're three-quarters of the way there!

Nicolette: Yes, Daddy, that's *Dominic's* thing to say!

Father: Well, I've said it now.

Nicolette: But that's not fair, Daddy! You say: "I hope to God there's not going to be a holdup in Sudstow High Street."

Dominic: You've *spoilt* it, Daddy, you've *spoilt* it! You've said my thing!

Nicolette: Now you've made Dominic cry.

Father: Calm down, Dominic. Be your age.

Dominic: How would you like it if I said your things? How would you like it if I said "A site for sore eyes"?

Mother: Don't be disrespectful to your father, Dominic.

Dominic: I don't care! *A site for sore eyes! A site for sore eyes! A site for sore eyes!*

Mother: If you don't stop this instant, Dominic, I'm going to. . . .

Nicolette: Daddy, Daddy! We've gone past Cook and Cook (Wholesale Tobacconists) and you haven't said your joke about spoiling the breath!

Father: Oh, dry up.

Mother: Now they're both howling. It's all your fault, John. They just copy you.

Father: That's what you always say.

Mother: And that's what *you* always say!

Father: Well, all I can say is, I hope to God there's not going to be a holdup in Sudstow High Street.

The Tale of Tiny TIM

I know what I want for Christmas. I want a collected edition of those roguish articles that appear about now in the various Christmas supplements telling you how to recover from drinking yourself sick.

"Some connoisseurs of the screaming abdabs," they simper manfully, "swear by a mixture of angostura bitters and Condy's fluid for bringing their red-hot eyeballs back out of orbit." Oh, what fun, fun, fun it is, men, planning it all in advance!

No, I'm just trying to look like one of the boys (though as a matter of fact I shouldn't mind having a reliable nausea cure around right now to recover from reading the Christmas supplements). What I really want, please, Father Christmas, is a watch I saw advertised in the *New York Times* recently. "Not just a watch," said the slogan. "A whole Public Relations campaign in itself."

This is the toy for me. I see it as being a miracle of horological craftsmanship—a sort of cuckoo-watch, only instead of a cuckoo popping out to tell you the time, there would be a series of merry dwarf public relations consultants.

"How jolly nice to see you, Mike!" cries the first of the seven snow-white dwarfs—I think his name's Creepy—giving one a tiny but immensely firm handshake. "I've arranged this little get-together because I've got some news about the time which I thought might interest you. I can't give you the actual figures, of course, but you can take my word for it that at the third stroke the time will be absolutely bang up to the minute."

The next time the watch chimes it's Creepy's colleague Crumby who pops out—accompanied by a tiny snow-white model girl in fish-net stockings. "I thought she might make rather a juicy angle on the time, old man," said Crumby. "I'll have her photographed for you, with a caption reading: 'Who wants to forget the time, when there's a striking clock like this around! Lovely Romaine Roxy (.038 in.-.024 in.- .038 in.) doesn't look slow to us, so watch it, boys! The lady's got time on her hands!'"

An hour later another hard-working little fellow pops out, Breezy, armed with a tiny handout starting: "Shakespeare describes midnight as 'the witching hour,' but there need be nothing unpleasant about 12 o'clock these days with a skilled consultant to handle the announcement. . . ." He also has a tiny list of historically interesting times of day—4.30 p.m., outbreak of Second Punic War; 10.12 a.m. official opening of the Diet of Worms, etc.—and a beautifully worked minia- ture photograph of Romaine Roxy being crowned Miss Eight o'Clock by Kingsley Amis.

"Vodka or whisky, Mike?" says Boozy, the next tiny figure to emerge. "Have another one. No, it's on me. Now, look, it's more than my job's worth to tell you what the time is now, old boy. Same again? Frankly, old boy, I'd take it as a great favour if you'd let this one ride. Know what I mean? Have another. Good old Mike—you're a real pal. One for the road—no, I insist. I know you won't let me down on this one, Mike."

Before one has a chance to wind the thing up the little trapdoor flies open again and Fishy pops out. Fishy is an exact reproduction in miniature of a well-known Conservative M.P. "The time has come," he says, "for us to stand up and declare, without fear or equivocation, that the hour has struck." With that he launches the Free Timekeeping Group, and sets to work to persuade fellow M.P.s at discreet lunch parties in the Palace of Westminster that the time is 10.30 p.m. Once they have got it on the Statute Book that this is the time, it will be learnt with great surprise that Fishy is a director of a tiny company that makes watches and clocks with their tiny hands stuck permanently at 10.30.

"Of course you want to know the time," says Wishful, who darts out next, his tiny eyes glowing with sympathetic liberal indignation. "You don't want any of this public relations flim-flam. You want the facts. I'll move heaven and earth to get them for you, Mike. I'm on your side, believe me. That's what I'm here for. Look, why don't we meet for lunch next week and really get down to it?"

Finally Cock, the President of the Institute of Dwarf Public Relations Consultants, puts in a minuscule appearance. He makes a vigorous miniature protest against the campaign of ill-informed calumny being waged in certain quarters against him and his colleagues. They perform an essential function in the modern world, he says. A watch is a complex piece of machinery. Have the critics ever stopped to consider how they would set about finding out the time from it without the skilled intercession of Creepy, Crumby, Breezy, Boozy, Fishy, Wishful, and Cock?

In an attempt to remove misunderstanding he sets up a tiny public relations committee to put the dwarfs' case. Only, unfortunately, there turns out to be so much misunderstanding of the public relations committee that it has to set up a public relations sub-committee to explain *its* case. And, of course, the public relations sub-committee comes up against such a mass of prejudice that it has to appoint a public relations sub-sub-committee. . . .

Whereas

(A) The Author of this Deed is at present seised in fee simple and in stupor tremens by the process of moving house.

(B) The Author is of sound mind SAVE THAT the Vendor of the first part and the Mortgagee of the second part and the Assignor of the third part and the Leaseholder of the fourth part and the Lessee of the fifth part and the Curtainor of the sixth part and the Carpetee of the seventh part and the Gasholder of the eighth part HAVE AGREED to cover all floors walls tables and other surfaces in the present residence of the Author with three coats of prime quality LEGAL DOCUMENTS.

(C) The aforementioned legal documents are close carpeted throughout with verbiage of a tasteful period character.

Provided that
A space shall be kept clear among the said verbiage to accommodate an Excise Stamp charged at NOT MORE than one third of the Government's current defence expenditure.

And wherethemore
(A) For a consideration the Solicitors of the aforementioned parties have agreed to join in these deeds SEEING THAT no aforementioned party would really go with a swing without them.

(B) Given the slightest additional consideration the Solicitors' Solicitors and the Solicitors' Solicitors' Solicitors would doubtless also join in both in fee simple and fee compound.

Provided that
The aforementioned partygiver (hereinafter called "the Mortgaged Soul") shall not be responsible for maintaining

more than half the country's legal profession at any one time.

And wherewithstanding
IN THE EVENT of a person being both Vendor of one property
and Vendee of another it is required by Logic that the Market
cannot be unfavourable to him in both capacities.

EXCEPT THAT in the case of the Author the Market shall be
guaranteed to be permanently against him whether as Vendor
Vendee or Vendsoever.

And whereasmuchas
(A) The Friends of the Author (hereinafter called Christopher
and Lavinia Crumble) bought purchased or became seised of
their demesne two years ago for the sum of ONE THOUSAND
POUNDS (£1,000).

(B) The value of the said demesne THEREUPON without let
or hindrance and without prejudice to the liberal reputation
of the aforesaid Christopher and Lavinia Crumble rose to
TEN THOUSAND POUNDS (£10,000).

(C) This being achieved in part by the application of two
coats of pale mauve paint by the said Christopher Crumble
and in part by the removal of all adjacent tenants of immoral
or drunken habits or small means and their replacement by
new tenants of immoral or drunken habits and more substantial
means.

And wheremoresoever
Even those Friends of the Author known as Horace and Doris
Morris ordinarily situate in the same boat as the Author and
generally supposed by the Author to be at least as fee simple
about these matters as himself have acquired a residence the
size of a small cathedral for A SONG (1 Sng.).

And wherewithas
(A) In contradistinction to the Morrises and Crumbles the

Author of this Deed (or Doer or Deedee) shall entertain all reasonable certainty that he will hereinafter be known as the Deedled or Done.

(B) The Author shall hereupon feel himself personally responsible for the maintenance in good condition of the Property Market heretofore known as the Property Racket.

(C) The Author shall be absolutely entitled to feel ground floor flat by the whole business.

Now it is agreed

The Author shall have in perpetuity the peaceful enjoyment of the dirty end of the stick.

Now this deed

WITNESSETH as follows:

The Author solemnly covenants with himself that notwithstanding overcrowding dilapidation infestation sudden enrichment sudden impoverishment conjugal representations or the purchase by Horace and Doris Morris of a royal palace in good order for fifteen shillings and sixpence NOR EVEN WITHSTANDING unemployment need and hunger among the Legal Profession HE SHALL before he contemplates moving house again meditate deeply upon this document for three calendar months following the first full moon after the penultimate Quarter Day of the next Leap Year but one.

In witness whereof the party hereto sets hereunder his exhausted hand.

Total Scholarship

I was delighted to hear

I was depressed to see

I was interested to learn that the complete works of the late Charlie Parker, the great master of modern jazz, are being brought out in a variorum edition, including all the false starts and alternative readings.

It surprises me

It does not surprise me

It surprises me that no one has yet suggested publishing a variorum edition of any journalist's works. I should think they must get round to it finally.

As a matter of fact, I have given the matter a certain amount / a great deal of thought, and I am rather inclined / absolutely resolved to make a start in that direction myself. For the benefit of posterity I am going to begin writing my own footnotes.[1] I'm going to stop / cease / desist from crossing out the speeling[2] mistakes, and thoughtlessly chucking / casually flinging / irresponsibly precipitating the material I don't use into the waste-paper basket.[3] In a word,

[1] This is a good example of the *genre*.

[2] Mis-spelling for *spieling*—"persuasive talking."

[3] Reichart remarks that "basket" was a common euphemism in the Royal Navy *c.*1930 for "bastard," and suggests that by analogy with debased Anglo-Indian usages such as "janker-wallah" the phrase "waste-paper basket" may perhaps be understood as "salvage collector." But more probably in this context, "a receptacle for waste-paper."

I'm going to compile my *own* ~~voriarum[4]~~ ~~viarorum[5]~~ variorum edition. It'll save somebody[6] a lot of work, anyway.

James Thurber[7] once remarked that if you saw his first drafts you'd think the cleaning woman[8] had written them. If his first drafts really could have provoked scholars to suppose anything so stimulating to literary research, they were source-material which it was wanton vandalism of Thurber to throw away.[9]

DON'T FORGET RING CRUMBLE ABOUT DINNER THURS*!!!!*[10]

This new approach represents a serious criticism of our recieved (check spelling)[11] idea of the function of art. From a superficial point of view, it has always seemed that the whole point of books, articles, poems, and so forth was their form and subject.[12] It has been left to modern scholarship to show that their real significance lies in the light which they cast upon their authors.

In other words

To put it slightly differently

Otherwise speaking (Is this English?)[13] a creative under-

---

[4]*Voriarum:* corruption of *vomitorium.*

[5]*Viarorum:* i.e., via Rorum. Rorum is a non-existent place, therefore, "by way of nowhere," i.e., "not by any means" (humorous usage).

[6]Exactly whom is a matter of speculation. Reichart suggests that he himself is intended here, but Skimming disputes this.

[7]James Grover Thurber (1894-1961).

[8]The so-called "Dark Lady of the Broom Cupboard." Identified by Skimming as Della (cf. Thurber: "My World and Welcome To It"). Pilsudsky's theory that it was the Earl of Arran is not generally accepted.

[9]Probably intended jocularly, but the simple truth none the less.

[10]Meaning obscure. For an interesting explanation in Jungian terms, see Rosie (Journ. of Amer. Soc. of Ephem. Lit., vol XXIII).

[11]It is typical of the author's "feel" for language that he sensed this word was mis-spelt.

[12]This observation has been confirmed by many other authorities, e.g. Westland, Boosey, Sidgwick, Fanfani and da Costa.

[13]No.

taking is nothing less than the autobiography of the undertak

That is to say, art is interesting because it tells us about the artists[14]—who are of course interesting because they produce ar

In other words, the whole of art is nothing less than a running gossip column on the art world.[15]

[14]Very true.

[15]This pungent and devastating conclusion is of the greatest interest because of the light it sheds on the author's ability to reach, in this case, a pungent and devastating conclusion.

What the Peepers See

A perpetual state of conflict and unrest exists between my eyes and the printed word. To be blunt, my eyes do not find words congenial co-workers in the business of communication.

It's not the fault of the words, which are patient and long-suffering in the face of constant abuse. It's my eyes. They won't settle down to do one job at a time; they're slapdash; they jump to conclusions; and they're highly counter-suggestible. Speaking for the management, I can tell you they're a right pair of layabouts.

They read MACMILLAN PUTS PARTY'S TRUST IN HOME as MACMILLAN PUT PARTLY TRUSSED IN HOME. With salacious agility they leap five paragraphs of life-enhancing descriptive prose to the erotic events they have miraculously detected at the bottom of the next page.

They read magazines backwards, jumping unsteadily back through the country notes and the annual reports of holding company holding companies, and give out exhausted long before they reach MIXED MANNING: A CAUTIOUS REASSESSMENT? at the front.

They're at their very worst with the eight daily newspapers that face them each morning. The rich profusion of sizes and styles and arrangements exhibited by the words in the newspapers completely demoralises them. They run hopelessly back and forth from one story to another like panic-stricken chickens. And yet they're so hidebound by restrictive practices that even at this juncture they refuse to see more than one size of type at a time—if they see the small headlines they don't see the large ones, and if they see the text they don't see the headlines at all.

Heavens, it makes me mad to think of all the time and ingenuity the printers and sub-editors have expended to make life easy for the readers' eyes—only to have ungrateful young peepers like mine pick and choose and complain. But isn't that the modern pupil all over? All they think of is eye, eye, eye.

With typical cowardly idleness they always start by picking on the smallest type at the bottom of the page, hoping no doubt that my hand will absent-mindedly turn the page over before they come up against anything their own size.

Short of pinning the newspaper to the wall, and slowly advancing from the other side of the room with my glasses off, reading it line by line like an oculist's chart, I suppose I'm condemned to go on starting the front page each morning with the *This Funny Old World* section at the bottom:

HIS PET ATE—TROUSERS

Harold Morbidly (47) went to work in his underpants after his pet hamster, Lulu, ate his trousers, Chingford, Essex, magistrates were told yesterday.

Discouraged by this inauspicious intelligence, my eyes labour slowly up from the bottom of the next column along.

Last night a man was helping the police in their inquiries.

"I tried to stop him," said Mrs. Sough, "by running after him shouting 'Help, police!'"

He grabbed the money from the till and ran out of the shop. Then he pulled out a gun and said, "This is a stick-up."

"So of course," said Mrs. Sough, "I assumed he was a perfectly ordinary customer. . . ."

It doesn't make any sense to me. Hey, just a moment—didn't I catch a glimpse of "intimacy occurred" seven columns over to the left somewhere? Ah, here we are.

. . . An opportunity to show the Prime Minister knew the North-East with considerable intimacy occurred when. . . .

Oh. H'm. Where was I?

"The morals of young people today," said Sir Harold Sidewinder . . .

That wasn't it, was it?

. . . are to be either scrapped or put into mothballs.

Nor that. Where the devil was it?

HEAVY LASSES KEEP GIANT COMPANY IN BED

No.

"The morals of young people . . ."

What? Heavy lasses do *what?* Where did I see that? Oh, HEAVY LOSSES KEEP GIANT COMPANY IN RED. Yes. Heavens, I'm bored. Must try and stagger a bit higher, though.

. . . wiped out. First reports put the number of dead and missing at . . .

Funny about those heavy lasses, I must say.

. . . when disaster struck . . . many thousands rendered homeless . . .

What was that rather amusing story about a hamster going into mothballs? Forgotten already. More or less squeezed this page dry, haven't I? Just glance at the main headline . . .

. . . and I can turn over. Nothing in the damned paper, as usual.

I don't know what the solution is. Perhaps lead the page with HAMSTER INCIDENT SHOCK and make the tailpiece at the bottom

Page One Fun

WELL, I DECLARE . . . !

"I declare war on Russia," said Sir Alec Douglas-Home (60) opening a Staggered Hours exhibition yesterday. Experts combing the radio-active rubble of London last night believed that what Sir Alec really said was not "Russia" but "rush-hour."

My eyes would get round it somehow, though. Probably start reading the *advertisements*.

51 To Blangy

Another kilometre stone coming up . . . 51 to Blangy-le-Duc. Superb views on either side of the road, any of which we could stop and look at if we chose. Delightful sensation of being captain of one's own destiny. Muse on therapeutic effect car has on human ego. One's choice potential is extended, and . . . Become conscious of wife asking question. Stop musing. Listen.

"*. . . just thinking why don't we stop along here somewhere and look at the view, dear?*"

Stop? Of course. Could easily, anywhere. With so many superb views, only difficulty to know where. Not *there*, obviously—right next to electric pylon. And not *there*, clearly —two cars there already. Now a very narrow bit with nowhere to pull off the road. Just get this stretch over and look again.

Now, slow. *That* spot would have been all right anywhere else, but not quite as good as some of the places we passed a mile or two back. What's that hooting behind? Good God, lorry I overtook five minutes ago trying to overtake me! Damned liberty! If I go back to my normal speed, like this, you'll realise what a big mistake you're making, my friend.

"*That looked quite a good place.*"

"What? Oh, I didn't see it. Not worth going back, is it?"

Rather dull stretch here. Kilometre post coming up. Still 48 kilometres to Blangy-le-Duc. H'm. Now 11.30, so must have been averaging scarcely 60 kilometres an hour since St.-Sévère. If it's the same sort of road ahead, that means we shan't be at Blangy until about 12.15. Then it's about, say,

70 kilometres from Blangy to Le Hoquet—say, 1.30. Then, say, half an hour for . . .

"*Aren't you going to stop, then?*"

Um? Stop?"

. . . half an hour for lunch. Say two o'clock. Then round about 100 kilometres from Le Hoquet to Pisaller. Say . . .

"*To look at the view.*"

"What view? Rather seedy bit here."

. . . say four o'clock, allowing a bit of time in hand, which will give us about two hours to get down to Uze . . .

"*Perhaps we ought to stop in Blangy instead, then.*"

"Is there something we ought to see there?"

"*Fifteenth-century castle, Romanesque cathedral,* musée gastro-nomique, *and traditional slipper-weaving industry.*"

Just a moment, what does that kilometre stone say? Blangy 45. Must stop looking at kilometre stones. Tedious obsession. Still, done those three kilometres in just under three minutes. If we kept that up we'd make Blangy at say 12.5, and Le Hoquet at . . .

"*What do you think?*"

"What? Oh, yes. Yes."

. . . Le Hoquet at, say, 1.15. Though not if we're stopping at Blangy, of course. Forgotten that. Throws the whole calculation right out.

"We don't want to stop very long at Blangy, do we?"

"*We ought to look at it for a bit, oughtn't we?*"

Let's see. Say 10 minutes for the Romanesque cathedral, 10 minutes for the museum, five minutes for the castle—oh, say about 30 minutes altogether. Here's another kilometre stone coming up. Won't look this time. Well, perhaps just this once. 43! Two kilometres in two and a half minutes! That means we shan't be at Blangy until about 12.20, and if we stop for half an hour, that means 2.10, no, 2.20

at Le Hoquet and . . . Must explain all this carefully to wife.

"I was just thinking, we don't really want to look round a museum in this heat, do we? What do you think?"

"*What do you think?*"

Cut the museum, then. After all, we've got 170 solid kilometres to do between Blangy and Pisaller. What's that in miles? Multiply by eight and divide by five; 270 miles. 270 miles! God, it can't be! Can it?

"I was thinking, perhaps we ought to give the traditional bedsock factory a miss. After all, we did spend at least half an hour looking round Cahiers yesterday. No one could accuse us of—well, I don't know, whatever anyone might start accusing us of. What do you think?"

"*I don't know. What do you think?*"

Cut the bedsock works, then. That saves us, what, 15 minutes? So we should reach Le Hoquet at . . . Did I say 270 miles? I must have meant 170 miles, or 270 kilometres. Mustn't I? Still, either way . . .

"We saw a Romanesque cathedral yesterday at Cahiers, didn't we?"

"*Did we? I thought it was a Gothic bell-tower we saw at Cahiers?*"

Gothic bell-tower? Gothic bell . . . Watch out, another kilometre stone coming up. No, no! Must stop looking at the damn things!

"*Perhaps you'd rather not stop at Blangy at all, dear?*"

"Of course we must stop there. We don't want to go charging across the country without ever seeing anything, do we? We're not in a charabanc. It's just that I don't want to spend the whole damned holiday looking at Romanesque cathedrals, that's all . . ."

"*Two in ten days is scarcely . . .*"

"Two? What was that thing we drove past in the rain at Grince? Wasn't that a Romanesque cathedral?"

Have to stop at Blangy for petrol, anyway. Will it see us through the 270 kilometres to Pisaller if we get 20 litres, plus the gallon and a half in the tank now, less the 40 kilometres from here to Blangy at 38 miles per gallon? Let's see, 20 divided by about $4\frac{1}{2}$, plus $1\frac{1}{2}$ minus 40 times 5 divided by 8 multiplied by 38. No, no. . . .

"*Look out, dear!*"

"All right, all right. I could see him perfectly well, I assure you."

Do it the other way round. 38 times 8 over 5 divided by $4\frac{1}{2}$. . . . Hold on, another kilometre stone. STOP LOOKING AT THE KILOMETRE STONES! You're going mad! Look at the goddam countryside like a normal human being!

I suppose if it's a fifteenth-century castle. . . . Perhaps we could just find a petrol station where we could see the castle without getting out of the car. Now, say we stopped for 10 minutes. In English minutes, that's 10 times 5 over 8, say $6\frac{1}{4}$ minutes. Or do I mean 16 kilominutes? If I could just work that out in cathedrals per litre. . . .

Word Sanctuary

From Lord Disgusted

Sir,—I must crave your indulgence for addressing you in this style. It is, I suppose, somewhat unusual in conversation, but after all these years the epistolary form is the one in which I feel myself most at home, even chatting to a journalist like yourself whom I am entertaining to lunch.

I am surely not alone, Sir, in finding that while sticks and stones may break my bones, words can give me apoplexy. Unless I have been intolerably misinformed from my childhood up, the English language, its vocabulary, syntax, and spelling, were given us by God in their present form as an uplifting discipline. Mis-spellings, split infinitives, and neologisms I take as calculated affronts to my whole moral code.

As you know, I have devoted a considerable part of my life to hunting them down and dragging them into the Letters to the Editor columns, manacled to the orotund ironies of my own entirely correct prose-style. It has not been an easy vocation; I have had to hold myself ready to be outraged at all hours. The high moral tone I have been able to enjoy, however, has not been entirely without its satisfactions. A little more roast beef?

But I digress. Neologisms, I find, are the outrages the most likely to provoke a rise in blood pressure. New words! What the devil do we want new words for? Illegitimately formed, as like as not, half Latin and half Greek, by some semi-literate scientist to denote some damned piece of modern nonsense the rest of us do not wish to know about. A lot of canting jargon! Is the language of Shakespeare and Milton not good enough for some twopenny little nuclear nobody to blow us all to Kingdom Come with?

Perhaps I should make it clear that I am myself an Arts man. To a scientist, I suppose, words are unimportant, merely adjuncts to blowing things up. But to me words are essential tools without which I could not write my Letters to the Editor. I may say that I think the scientists have an infernal impertinence in interfering with my work, and a diabolical arrogance in inventing new words, when I, the generally recognised guardian of the language, should not dream of altering it by a hair's breadth.

But the Beelzebub of neologisms, Sir, is the Americanism. Let me ask a plain question. Whose language is it? Ours or theirs? It makes me furious when I see our own language larded with words like "editorialise" and "hospitalise." Cannot people say "give as an opinion in an editorial" and "cause to go to hospital"? Are they too lazy to say the extra syllables? Are they too sunk in moral torpor to work out the proper syntax?

And "commuter"! Every time I hear the word "commuter" I see a red haze of rage in front of my eyes. It is an entirely unnecessary outrage, since there is a perfectly good English expression: "A man who lives in one place and works in another, and who travels back and forth between the two each day." There is simply no need for a new word. A man who lives in one place and works in another, and who travels back and forth between the two each day, is simply a man who lives in one place and works in another, and who travels back and forth between the two each day—and that is all there is to say about it.

It might be asked—though so far as I know it never has

been—what is wrong with incorrect English. Surely anyone who has ever learnt any moral standards at all knows in his heart that "Don't mention it" is right and that "You're welcome" is wrong. One should think of words as applicants for positions of sacred trust in one's employment. Naturally one inquires into their backgrounds, and if they turn out to be foreigners, like "You're welcome," or of questionably mixed stock, like "telecast" (ugh!), then one naturally thinks twice about employing them.

At a time like this, when our country is being attacked on all sides, the correctness of our language is more important than ever. If we thought of ourselves as being at all times on parade, if we tightened up the nation's spelling, ruthlessly stamped out split infinitives and hanging participles, and prohibited the manufacture or import of any new word whatsoever, unless designed by a qualified man like myself with a proper classical education, we could soon show our detractors where we stood in the world.

If I had my way, our security organisations would be employed to examine the antecedents of every word and expression in the language. Sometimes perfectly innocent-looking phrases one uses oneself turn out to be quite unacceptable when one looks into them. One of my colleagues pointed out in a Letter to the Editor recently that the expression "Have you got a . . . ?" is being replaced by "Do you have a . . . ?"—and that the latter, which one might in all innocence have entertained on one's own lips, is of American extraction! As soon as one knows, of course, one can hear just how morally objectionable it is. But if the public had not been warned, the lovely English word "got" would have been quietly murdered.

But to come to the point, Sir. I trust you will join the organisation I am founding, the Council for the Preservation of Verbal England. I expect massive support from all the columnists, humourists, school teachers, and writers of Letters to the Editor who have already cared so much and so long. Help us to set an example to *hoi polloi* by returning to our *lares et penates*—a close *rapport* with the *Urgeist* of the English language.

And so, unless you would like another cup of coffee, I remain, Sir,

Yours, etc.
Disgusted

On the Subject of Objects

I expect you're pretty used to people lying here in your consulting-room and telling you the most terrible things about themselves, aren't you, Dr. Wienerkreis? I mean, thinking they've got all sorts of frightful things wrong with them which turn out to be nothing but . . . ?

Yes, well, anyway, the point is, Dr. Wienerkreis, I'm suffering from, I mean, I think I might possibly have got a . . . well, *a serendipity deficiency.*

I mean, I never *find* things. Everyone I know but me seems to find things. What sort of things? Well, they find, sort of, *objects.* They come across fantastic sea-shells on the beach. They stumble on oddly shaped pieces of wood in fields. They glance into a junk shop and pick up an elegant brass letter balance for seven-and-six, say, or an amusing Victorian steel engraving for tenpence-halfpenny. Well, you know, *objects.*

What? Well, they take them home and arrange them as it were casually in their living-rooms. What do they do then? Well, I suppose they look at them. I mean, they're intriguing things. I suppose they look at them and feel intrigued. When they have guests the guests look at them and feel intrigued.

For example, we have some friends called the Crumbles. When one goes into the Crumbles' living-room one's surrounded on all sides by patch-boxes, astrolabes, sticks of Victorian rock, model Dreadnoughts, lumps of quartz-porphyry, eighteenth-century milking stools, Chinese toothpicks. One's intrigued. It gives one something to talk about.

What does one say? Well, I don't know, one says perhaps *"What's this intriguing little object, then?"* Something like that.

And Christopher Crumble says, more or less, "*That? Oh, that's an early Georgian dentist's forceps I found by sheerest chance at a little shop I know down in Devizes.*" Or something along those lines. Well, then you're away on a sort of whimsical-cultural, or cultural-whimsical, conversation that will see you through until the soup's on the table.

I know, I know. . . . Of course I don't think *everyone* collects intriguing objects. Some people collect beer-mats and miniature liqueur bottles. Some people collect Louis XV candle-snuffers or Baroque door-knobs. But the people I know are too sophisticated for beer-mats and too poor for Baroque door-knobs. So they collect amusing objects. The point is, Dr. Wienerkreis, I have a social context I have to try to fit into.

The trouble is, the fields I walk through are just full of earth. Whenever I look into a junk shop the contents consist exclusively of junk. I never see any amusing Victorian ship's chronometers. All I see is heaps of rusty ice-skates, broken clockwork trains, warped rattan cake-stands, and chipped mauve cocktail sets that someone got for 1,700 cigarette tokens in 1938. The only thing I've ever found anywhere is the word *serendipity*, which I came across by absolute chance in a little dictionary I know. . . .

Yes, of course it matters. When the Crumbles come to dinner with us they're surrounded by great quantities of nothing. Yes, nothing at all. Well, to be absolutely precise, I suppose there are usually a few things lying around like plastic giveaways out of cereal packets, week-old copies of the *Daily Mirror*, broken sunglasses, bits of paper with "No milk Sunday" written on them, that sort of thing.

I mean, our living-room is a cultural desert. You can't expect people to say "*Where did you get this intriguing little 'Daily Mirror' from?*" You can't show guests the plastic television personalities, and explain how you just picked them up by sheerest chance as they fell out of a little Fungles packet you know down behind the refrigerator.

Of course, the plastic television personalities may come to be amusing objects in time. By the turn of the century the graciously ageing Crumbles may well have a small but distinguished collection of them in their living-room, together with an amusing old wireless valve, a highly intriguing Dun-in-a-Jiff patent potato peeler (c. 1960), and a number of nostalgically beautiful and rather valuable photographs from *Reveille* of *le pin-up de cheesecake* school. Not us, though—we'll just have a couple of week-old numbers of the *Times-Mirror* and some broken bits of the central-heating reactor lying on the floor.

I need help, Dr. Wienerkreis. Help myself? You mean, practise? Start off modestly and work up to normal serendipity by easy stages?

I see what you mean. I could begin by arranging the old *Daily Mirrors* and the broken sunglasses in a tasteful way. Is that the sort of thing you have in mind? Then I could try finding slightly unusual looking pebbles and bits of twig. I could buy some of the less rusty ice-skates and the less chipped mauve cocktail-shakers. Then I could gradually work back through 1930s toothbrush-holders, 1920s false teeth, and Edwardian rubber dog-bones, to Diamond Jubilee shoe-trees and Great Exhibition bradawls.

But Dr. Wienerkreis, I have a bad block here—I'd feel such a damned fool having an Edwardian rubber dog-bone about the house without having an Edwardian dog to chew it. Do you think I'd get over that? I'm afraid I might retreat into gross psychotic delusion—decide I was the only one who was sane, and start writing articles trying to make everyone else feel a damned fool for not feeling a damned fool.

Divine *News, Darlings!*

Among the aristocracy, reports a man at Glasgow University who has been studying their ways, one marriage in every four now ends in divorce. In other words, the aristocracy have reached the status of a Problem, and the Bishop of Twicester and I are deeply concerned about it.

"I am convinced," he writes in a helpful little booklet entitled *The Aristocracy Today: a Challenge and an Opportunity*, "that there is nothing fundamentally wrong with modern aristocrats. We hear a lot about the bad ones, but at heart most of them are perfectly decent and uncommonly high-spirited folk.

"The trouble is, they lack leadership. They have plenty of money to spend, and they're subjected to all sorts of unscrupulous commercial pressures. A regular barrage of suggestive advertising screams class, class, class at them seven days a week. Do we wonder they sometimes take the wrong turning?

"Those of us who go among them to any extent know how resentful they are of ill-informed criticism, and how lost and bewildered they feel in a world which seems to be run entirely for the benefit of their inferiors. My work takes me into a large club for lords and ladies in the parish of Westminster, and I know from personal experience how very likeable and human some of them can be. In a club like this, where they are given proper facilities for self-expression, there is very little hooliganism or other delinquency."

The Bishop and I believe that the Church isn't getting through to the aristocracy because it doesn't really speak their language. All this "thou" and "thee" and "yeah, yeah, yeah," mean nothing at all to the average lord. And many of the teachings of the Church—particularly those that lay stress on poverty and humility—seem to have little relevance to life as they know it.

We feel that the only reason so many lords hang about racecourses and grouse moors is that they have nowhere else to go. They drink and gamble and inflict suffering on animals because they're bored. We want to see more clubs set up for them along the lines of the one at Westminster. It doesn't take much—some red leather upholstery and a begged or borrowed woolsack—to turn the average church crypt into a very gay and inviting little House of Lords, where the local nobility can enjoy soft drinks together and take part in constructive activities such as debating.

These clubs should be places where lords and ladies can feel at home in the sort of clothes they like to wear—which may mean anything from baggy tweeds to the full traditional "gear" of robes and coronets! Sober citizens may sniff, but very smart some of them can look, believe me, when they're "dressed to kill" at the local meet!

Above all, we want to encourage the lords and ladies to do their divorcing in a healthy, open atmosphere of camaraderie and good fellowship, and get right away from the old hole-and-corner approach. Let all the questions and worries be thrashed out fully and frankly. "Can pre-marital divorce ever be right?" "Will I lose my husband if I refuse to divorce him?" You'll be amazed at the things that worry these high-spirited old families.

But this by itself is not enough—we must try to attract them into the churches. The Bishop made a remarkable start last Sunday by holding a Lord and Lady Day Service. He decorated the Cathedral with sporting prints, and replaced the choir and organist with Debrett Dansant and his Debs Delights, who rendered a number of hymns which the Bishop had translated into straightforward upper-class English, such as "Too super, too dishy, too marvellous Chap!"

His Lordship himself galloped in on horseback, wearing hunting pink and plus-fours. Crying "View halloo!" he threw a gun into his shoulder, gave the angels in the roof a right and a left, and brought down a cock and a hen. Pausing only to set the port circulating among the congregation, he got the Rural Dean to give him a leg up into the pulpit, where all the known tongues of dukes and of barons descended on him simultaneously, and he preached thus:

"My text today is from Ecclesiastes chapter 5 verse 12: 'The sleep of a labourin' man is sweet.' Or as we say, 'The sleep of a labourin' man is puddin'.'

"How true that is, what? I mean to say, sometimes we draw a covert for the meanin' of life, and it seems to double back and go to earth. I know I do, what? But when you go forth from here today I want you to bear in your hearts the knowledge that whenever things get too utterly ghastly, too absolutely filthington, you can always drop in on God for a quick spiritual snifter.

"You see, I like to think of prayer as a kind of spiritual grouse shootin'—a chance to get shot of the odd brace of grumbles. Yes, as I said in the Teenagers' Service last week, goin' out after the birds is as much a part of religion as toddlin' along to Vespers or Holy Communers. And doin' a ton in the Rolls is just about as religious as you can get short of actually goin' in for Holy Orders kit. I mean to say, what?

"To him who hearkeneth not to the voice of righteousness the consequences could be dashed desperate, not to say hellish. But the man who doth the best he can in the jolly old circs is likely to have a heavenly time, doncher know, what?

"Shall we Johann Sebastian kneelers-peelers?"

And the whole congregation—Mrs. Thrumley, Mrs. Arthur Upstreet, and the Lord Bishop's old mother—fell upon their knees and repented bitterly of the way of life that had brought them into that place.

Hard at Leisure

Sun. Free afternoon. Baby summarily incarcerated for nap. Two low patent leisure chairs set out in sunlight for wife and self. Can scarcely believe it! After all the holidays when rained, and all the sunny days when had to work, and all the sunny holidays when had to paint bathroom or visit Great-Uncle Alexander. Leisure at last indubitably about to occur!

Stretch self on low leisure chair with awe. Am wearing leisurewear shirt, leisurewear trousers, leisurewear shoes. Have suitable leisure reading to hand. Feel am cutting terrific figure—at last living up to example set by heroes of modern leisure whose pictures appear in leisure pages. Very pleased with self.

Only connection with mundane reality of everyday Frayn —small piece of banana left over from baby's lunch squashed on sole of leisurewear shoe. Possibility cannot be ruled out that small piece of squashed, mundane banana will soil unspotted sanctity of new leisure chair. Make bold sacrifice —take leisurewear shoes off. Reveal non-leisurewear socks. H'm. Never mind—man as profoundly imbued with leisure as self can carry off non-leisurewear socks without turning hair.

Open leisure reading. " 'In those days,' said Sir Edward, 'we enjoyed a far greater amount of leisure than we do in these busy times. . . .' " Dazzling white glare from page. Good Lord—have forgotten leisurewear sunglasses! Get up, put leisurewear shoes on again to guard against any other banana, strained spinach, or half-digested tit-bits left over from baby's lunch, and fetch them. Lower self luxuriously into low leisure chair, remove leisurewear shoes, and stretch out hand for leisure reading.

Find it difficult to believe at first, but am at last forced to recognise that I must have taken leisure reading with me when fetching sunglasses and put it down somewhere indoors. Sit up, pull leisurewear shoes on, and hoist self out of low leisure chair all over again.

Return with book. With wry smile for benefit of self, check have not left behind handkerchief, keys, penknife, or whatever. Ease self down into chair, and remove shoes. Now where was I? Ah, yes. " 'In those days,' said Sir Edward, 'we enjoyed a far greater amount of . . .' " Still something horribly wrong. What can be? No! Well, would you believe—it must have taken off sunglasses indoors to look for book. . . .

Shoes on. Get up from remarkably low leisure chair. Descend to chair level again with sunglasses, book, spare handkerchief, pencil-sharpener, driving licence, and everything else man of leisure might possibly want. Reject interrogative look from wife—am definitely not losing temper. Quickly start to read. " 'In those days,' said Sir Edward. . . ." Hey, didn't I buy some leisurewear sandals last summer? Why aren't I wearing them? What's the use of leisure if don't take opportunity to use all available leisure equipment?

Shoes on. Heave self up. Search whole establishment for sandals in vain. Find cache of winter leisurewear I couldn't find during winter. Hurl on floor and return to leisure. Wife looks at me again. Let her know in no uncertain terms am NOT getting irritated.

Descend into chair. Off shoes. Up book. " 'In those days,' said Sir Edward. . . ." Is memory playing tricks, or is this lad Sir Edward repeating himself? Suddenly strikes me why am so hot and sticky—tall, cool drink that stands at every leisure-lover's elbow in the leisure-pages is missing. On shoes. Up carcass. Ah! Delicate muscles in arms and shoulders beginning to show unhealthy signs of strain from all these backward press-ups. Whole body developing certain inelegant sag.

Return with luke-warm beer apiece. Ease self back into chair. Shoes off. " 'In those days,' said Sir Edward. . . ." Telephone ringing. Feel sorry for wife, having to jump up to answer phone on hot summer afternoon. " 'In those days,' said Sir Edward, 'we enjoyed. . . .' " Funny—telephone still ringing. Wife must be getting a bit slow off the mark these days. Lower book to see. Wife still sitting there! Has lowered her book. Is looking at me. I look at her. She looks at me. Decide to sit fast as practical demonstration of solidarity with women's struggle for equal status.

Turn back to book. " 'In those days,' said Sir Edward . . ." Wife still looking at me. Decide on second thoughts to restrict demonstration of solidarity to brief recital of egalitarian male swearing and cursing as haul self wearily to feet and pull on shoes. Lace on right shoe goes into knots. Cram foot halfway in and hobble off as fast as can. Telephone stops ringing.

Abseil panting and grunting back down to sea level. Kick shoes off. " 'In those days,' said Sir Edward. . . ." Terrible suspicion strikes me. Haven't I read this book before? Isn't it all about some poor old lad called Sir Edward somebody or-other, who tells blood-curdling tales about the cruel amount of leisure inflicted on him when he was young? Reach out for consoling swig of luke-warm beer. Discover have already drained whole glassful in moment of absent-mindedness without noticing it.

Childish cries from within, announcing end of leisure.

187

Stagger thankfully indoors, without stopping to find where shoes got kicked, stepping on molten chocolate biscuit en route, and collapse on inelegant chair. Shoulders sag. Head lolls inertly. Rib cage settles on to pelvis. Gaze vacantly into space with mouth open, taking well-earned rest.

The Case of the Missing Kinks

"My Lords, Ladies, and Gentlemen, pray silence for the Warden of the Kinque Ports!"

A thousand banqueters waited expectantly. From the kinquiest ports of the world they had come—from Hamburg, from Malaga, from Macao—to pay homage at the Guildhall in London to the kinquiest nation of them all, and to see the Warden declare open the Spring Collections of new British kinks.

Slowly the aged Warden rose to his feet.

"The new kinks!" he gasped. "They've all been stolen!"

*　　*　　*

"I gather we're up against something pretty big this time," said Sadie Streak, shaking her long blonde hair free from her black leather negligee.

"Big?" said Kurius Frisson, examining the reflection of his perfect elegance in his manically polished toe-caps. "A vast international conspiracy known as PLOT, duckie."

The latest and best-loved couple in modern kinkology were breakfasting quietly in The Kink, their cosy little penthouse home built entirely of black leather and two-way mirror. Did they love each other? wondered Sadie, as she ground out her cigarette in the remains of the gentleman's relish. The week before Kurius had bestowed a playful kiss in passing on the sole of her boot, and she had responded by dislocating his neck with an expert Japanese thumbhold. But was this love?

"PLOT's never troubled us much in the past," she said lazily.

As if in answer, the head of Sadie's black leather teddy bear slumped sickeningly sideways, its neck expertly broken by a high-velocity frozen nerve gas bullet!

*   *   *

Sadie changed into a black leather bikini and went out to do a little shopping. On the corner of Bond Street stood a one-legged Armenian wearing a kinky boot on his wooden leg. He beckoned to Sadie to follow him.

"I am vearing zis kinky boot," he explained when they had reached the comfortable seclusion of a shop selling inflatable dummy gigolos, "to keep ze police off my tail."

With quiet craftsmanlike pleasure, Sadie seized his tail in a secret Japanese tail-lock and tortured him until he handed over a black leather bag marked "Swag."

*   *   *

"It's a pretty nasty business, Kurius," said Sadie, who had changed into a rubber cocktail dress trimmed with six-inch steel buckles.

"Tell me," urged Kurius, as the well-loved pair pretended to examine a display of gentlemen's reducing corsets in a little shop off Greek Street.

"Well, some of the fiends we're up against are downright *normal*. You know what they do? They get hold of women. . . ."

"I don't want to hear, Sadie!"

"Oh, all right."

"No, tell me, tell me!"

"Well, they—listen, Kurius—they *marry them!*"

Kurius shuddered ecstatically.

"What a horrible, beautiful kink! But if anyone tried that on you, duckie, I'd change into my rubber fighting plus-fours as quick as lightning."

* * *

The scene shifts to Tangier, glamorous centre of top international dope-smugglers. It shifts again to the Piraeus, legendary haunt of fabulously beautiful cosmopolitan call-girls. . . .

This shifty behaviour does not go unremarked. As the scene shifts back once again to London, two inconspicuous men in raincoats shadow it from the airport to its hotel. . . .

* * *

The phone rang. Knowledgeably, Kurius Frisson picked it up.

"Zis is ze Prime Minister speaking, Mr. Frisson," said a sinister Levantine voice. "I vont you to go to ze top of ze Hilton Hotel carrying £19,000 in a hollow crutch, and climb into ze giant pulping-mill you vill find zere."

Something told Kurius that it was not the Prime Minister's voice. He chuckled inwardly, and decided to have a bit of fun.

Pausing only to stuff £19,000 into a hollow crutch, he went to the appointed place and climbed into the pulping mill. Immediately it started up! The last thing he was conscious of was a face looking in at him. It was Miss Butz, the proprietress of the gentlemen's corset shop!

Then every bone in his body was smashed. He was pulped

and ground into a fine powder and scattered in the east wind blowing over Hyde Park. He was—dead.

We draw a discreet break for commercials across the distressing scene.

* * *

With one bound Kurius Frisson was alive again!

"Thanks to hearing the commercial for Luxiphags, the cigarettes that make a new man of you," he explained to Sadie back at The Kink. "No, really, duckie, I loved every minute of it."

At that moment a secret trap-door beneath the sitchen kink flew open, and out stepped a man in traditional rubber ceremonial robes.

"The Warden of the Kinque Ports!" breathed Kurius.

With a revealingly normal snarl the Warden pulled a flame-thrower out of his thigh-boots. But already the old Japanese magic in Sadie's fingers was at work, and with a hnunch! hlmph! squoosh! aaaaaah! the Warden's head was tied to his heels with the remains of his jugular vein.

"Nice work, girlie," tittered Kurius. "It must have been the Warden who was disguised as Miss Butz on the Hilton roof, and Miss Butz who was in the bag marked 'Swag'."

"Where was Swag, then?"

"He was murdered by the Warden when he discovered that the Warden was really working for a Ghanaian spy-ring, stealing the plans for new kinks. Anyway, so much for PLOT."

"It all tied up in the end," quipped Sadie lightly, stroking Kurius's cheek with a jewelled spur.

"Quip me again, duckie," murmured Kurius dreamily. "Only this time a leetle harderkins."